New English Conversation Arts 1

MP3 파일
다운로드
www.hyungseul.co.kr
자료실

Michael A. Putlack
Hyonho Lee
Stephen Poirier

형설출판사
www.hyungseul.co.kr

Introduction

English is becoming more and more important every year. People use it while traveling, conducting business, and meeting their friends. They do this not only in places such as the United States, Canada, England, and Australia but also in Japan, China, Italy, and Spain. People also use English a considerable amount in Korea as the number of people who speak English in the country increases every year.

The objective of this book is to teach basic English conversation. By using this book and studying all 12 units, students should be able to reach this goal. They should also be able to carry on basic English conversations about a wide variety of topics. Each chapter focuses on different elements of grammar that are important to students of the English language. In addition, each chapter focuses on different topics. These topics are both important and interesting. Among them are locations, health, looks, and clothes. Students will discover that when they use English in their daily lives, they will often use the very language and grammar that is covered in this book.

This book is intended to be used in a classroom setting. However, it can also be used by those individuals who are interested in learning English alone. While studying this book does not guarantee fluency in English, it will provide readers with the basic fundamentals they need to get a solid basic knowledge of English. We wish students the best of luck as they pursue their studies of the English language.

Michael A. Putlack

Hyonho Lee

Stephen Poirier

Contents

Unit 1
What's your name?

1. Vocabulary

personal 개인적인	**That sounds ~** 그 말을 들으니 ~하다.
information 정보	**fun** 재미(있는)
full name 성명	**hobby** 취미
major 전공, 주요한	**musical instrument** 악기
It's nice to meet you. 만나서 반갑습니다.	**photography** 사진 기술
engineering 공학(분야의 일)	**homework** 숙제, 집에서 할 과제
blood type 혈액형	**subject** 과목, 주제
office worker 회사원	**flavor** 맛, 취미, 취향
hometown 고향	**spot** 지점, 위치
introduce 소개하다	**culture** 문화
free time 여가 시간	**rude** 무례한, 실례가 되는, 버릇없는
activity 활동	**impolite** 예의가 없는
favorite 가장 좋아하는 (것)	**vote** 투표하다

2. Let's Warm Up *Personal Information*

Write down your personal information.

First Name: Last Name:

Full Name:

Age: Job:

School: Major:

Email Address: Cell Phone Number:

3. Conversation 1 *Meeting People*

Listen to the conversation. Then, practice it with a partner.

Jason: Hello. I'm Jason. What's your name? ***Sumi***: My name is Sumi. It's nice to meet you. ***Jason***: It's nice to meet you, too. ***Sumi***: Where are you from, Jason? ***Jason***: I'm from Australia. ***Sumi***: What do you do? ***Jason***: I'm a student. How about you? ***Sumi***: I'm a student, too. My major is engineering.	***Jason***: 안녕. 난 제이슨이야. 네 이름은 뭐니? ***Sumi***: 내 이름은 수미야. 만나서 반갑다. ***Jason***: 나도 반가워. ***Sumi***: 제이슨, 넌 어디서 왔니? ***Jason***: 호주에서 왔어. ***Sumi***: 직업은? ***Jason***: 학생이야. 너는? ***Sumi***: 나도 학생이야. 내 전공은 공학 쪽이야.

4. Let's Learn More 1

A *Read the information below.*

Ask personal questions by using "What is your ~?" or "What's your ~?" Answer these questions by using "My ______________ is ~" or "It's ~."

Q: What is your name?	A: My name is Sumi.
Q: What is your major?	A: My major is engineering.
Q: What's your cell phone number?	A: It's 010-555-4242.
Q: What's your email address?	A: It's michael123@thismail.com.

Answer the questions. Then, talk with your partner.

B

1. What is your first name? ____________________
2. What's your last name? ____________________
3. What is your full name? ____________________
4. What's your job? ____________________
5. What is your major? ____________________
6. What's your cell phone number? ____________________
7. What is your email address? ____________________
8. What's your blood type? ____________________

Read the information below. Then, answer the questions.

C

Many personal questions do NOT use "What's your ~?" There are many other kinds of personal questions. Look at the following questions and answers:

Q: How old are you?	A: I am 20 years old.
Q: Where do you go to school?	A: I go to Dongyang Mirae University.
Q: What do you do?	A: I am a student. / I am an office worker.
Q: Can you tell me about your family?	A: There are 4 people in my family.
Q: Where are you from?	A: I'm from Singapore.
Q: Where is your hometown?	A: My hometown is London.
Q: Where do you live?	A: I live in Incheon.

1. How old are you? ____________________
2. Where do you go to school? ____________________
3. What do you do? ____________________
4. Can you tell me about your family? ____________________
5. Where are you from? ____________________
6. Where is your hometown? ____________________
7. Where do you live? ____________________

D *Introduce yourself to your group members. Write the answers.*

	Student 1	Student 2	Student 3
Name			
School/Major			
Cell Phone Number			
Email Address			
Hometown			

E *Circle the mistakes. Then, write the correct sentences.*

1. I live on Seoul. → ______________________
2. My am twenty-two years old. → ______________________
3. There are 6 families in my family. → ______________________
4. I'm from the Korea. → ______________________
5. My majoring is electronics. → ______________________
6. My blood type is AB type. → ______________________

F *Match the questions with the answers.*

1. What's your name?
2. Where do you live?
3. How old are you?
4. Can you tell me about your family?
5. Where do you go to school?
6. Where is your hometown?
7. What do you do?
8. What's your cell phone number?

A. I am 21 years old.
B. I am an engineer.
C. I go to Central University.
D. I live in Suwon.
E. It's 010-123-4567.
F. I'm Changhoon.
G. There are four people in my family.
H. I come from Busan.

5. Conversation 2 *Free-Time Activities and Favorites*

Minho: Do you like Korea, Tina?
Tina: Yes, it's really nice here.
Minho: What do you do in your free time?
Tina: I meet my friends in my free time. What do you do?
Minho: In my free time, I watch movies.
Tina: That sounds fun. What's your favorite movie?
Minho: My favorite movie is *Spiderman*. I love action movies.
Tina: Me, too. Let's watch a movie together some time.

Minho: 너 한국이 마음에 드니, 티나?
Tina: 응, 여기 참 좋아.
Minho: 여가 시간엔 뭐하니?
Tina: 여가 시간에는 친구들을 만나. 너는 뭐하니?
Minho: 난 여가 시간에 영화를 봐.
Tina: 그거 재미있겠다. 제일 좋아하는 영화가 뭔데?
Minho: 내가 가장 좋아하는 영화는 스파이더맨이야. 난 액션영화를 좋아해.
Tina: 나도 그래. 언제 영화나 같이 보자.

6. Let's Learn More 2

A *Read the information below.*

Free-Time Activities	**Hobbies**
meeting friends	painting
drinking	playing musical instruments
shopping	taking pictures (photography)
watching TV/movies	playing sports

Ask and answer questions about free-time activities and hobbies like this:

Q: What do you do in your free time?

A: I do my homework in my free time.
A: In my free time, I go shopping.

Q: What is your hobby?

A: My hobby is soccer.
A: My hobby is playing the piano.

B *Answer the questions. Then, talk to your group members.*

1. What do you do in your free time?

   a. ____________________

   b. ____________________

   c. ____________________

2. What's your hobby?

   a. ____________________

   b. ____________________

   c. ____________________

C *Read the information below. Then, answer the questions.*

People often ask about favorites. A favorite is the thing you like the most.

Q: What is your favorite subject? A: My favorite subject is English.

Q: What's your favorite flavor of ice cream? A: It's chocolate.

1. What is your favorite food? ____________________
2. What's your favorite music? ____________________
3. What is your favorite book? ____________________
4. What's your favorite sport? ____________________
5. What is your favorite color? ____________________
6. Where is your favorite vacation spot? ____________________
7. Who is your favorite movie star? ____________________
8. Who is your favorite teacher? ____________________

7. Let's Learn About Culture

A *Read the passage.*

Korean culture and American culture are very different. Some personal questions are fine in Korean culture. However, they are very rude in American culture. (They are also rude in Canadian, British, and Australian cultures.) For example, in Korea, "How old are you?" is a very important question. BUT... In American culture, it is an impolite question. In addition, in Korea, "Are you married?" is an okay question. BUT... In American culture, it is a bad question. In American culture, people also do not usually ask about religion, politics, family, or money. Those are often bad questions. Good questions are about sports, the weather, hobbies, free-time activities, and favorites.

한국 문화와 미국 문화는 매우 다르다. 한국 문화에서는 개인적인 질문을 해도 되지만, 미국 문화에서는 큰 실례가 된다 (캐나다, 영국, 호주 문화에서도 실례다). 예를 들어, 한국에서는 "나이가 어떻게 되세요?"가 중요한 질문이다. 그러나 미국 문화에서 이런 질문은 무례한 질문이다. 게다가 한국에서는 "결혼하셨어요?"라고 물어도 되지만, 미국 문화에서는 해서는 안 되는 질문이다. 또 미국 문화에서는 종교, 정치, 가족, 수입 등에 대해서 묻지 않는다. 그런 질문들은 바람직하지 않은 질문이 되는 경우가 많다. 바람직한 질문은 스포츠, 날씨, 취미, 여가 활동 및 좋아하는 일에 관한 것들이다.

B *Are these questions polite (P) or impolite (I) in American culture? Write the answers.*

1. ________ What is your religion?
2. ________ Why aren't you married?
3. ________ Who is your favorite baseball team?
4. ________ How do you like the weather?
5. ________ What do you do in your free time?
6. ________ How much money do you make?
7. ________ Who did you vote for?
8. ________ Do you have a hobby?

8. Use Your Knowledge

A *Look at the picture.*

B *Complete the questions and answers. Then, practice them with your partner.*

Person 1

1. What's your first name? ____________________
2. ____________________ I go to Harvard.
3. What's your hobby? ____________________
4. ____________________ It's 010-430-8547.

Person 2

1. ____________________ My name is Jenny Nelson.
2. What do you do? ____________________
3. What do you do in your free time? ____________________
4. What's your cell phone number? ____________________

Person 3

1. Where do you go to school? ____________________
2. What's your favorite subject? ____________________
3. ____________________ I go shopping in my free time.
4. What's your email address? ____________________

Unit 2
I'm doing my homework right now.

1. Vocabulary

busy 바쁜
have a test 시험을 치르다
together 함께
everyone 모든 사람들
classmate 반 친구
policeman 경찰관
chef 조리사
catch 잡다
bank robber 은행 강도
chase 뒤쫓다
take care of 돌보다
come back 돌아오다
patient 환자, 참을성 있는
call 부르다, 전화하다
practice 연습하다
pronoun 대명사
negative 부정적인
church 교회
surf the Internet 인터넷 검색하다
go on a picnic 소풍가다

anything 무엇이든지
chat online 온라인 채팅하다
buy a present 선물을 사다
finish 끝내다
plans 계획, 할 일, 약속 등
Why don't you ~? ~하지 그러니?
graduate 졸업하다
excited 기분 좋은, 흥분된
visit 방문하다
leave 떠나다, 출발하다, 남겨놓다

2. Let's Warm Up *Common Activities*

Look at the picture. What are they doing now?

1. The girl is ______________________________.
2. The boy is ______________________________.
3. The two students are ______________________________.

3. Conversation 1 *The Present Continuous Tense*

Listen to the conversation. Then, practice it with a partner.

Mark:	Hey, Changhoon. Are you busy now?
Changhoon:	Yes, I am.
Mark:	Really? What are you doing now?
Changhoon:	I'm doing my homework right now.
Mark:	I see. Then where is Tina? What is she doing?
Changhoon:	Tina is studying at the library. She has a test tomorrow.
Mark:	And Minho and Jason are playing basketball together.
Changhoon:	Everyone is busy. They are all doing something now.

Mark:	창훈아, 안녕. 지금 바쁘니?
Changhoon:	응, 바빠.
Mark:	그래? 뭐하는데?
Changhoon:	지금 숙제를 하고 있어.
Mark:	알았어. 그럼 티나는 어디 있니? 걔는 뭐해?
Changhoon:	티나는 도서관에서 공부해. 내일 시험이 있거든.
Mark:	민호와 제이슨은 함께 농구하고 있는데.
Changhoon:	다들 바쁘구나. 모두들 지금 뭔가를 하고 있어.

4. Let's Learn More 1

A *Read the information below.*

Use the present continuous tense (현재진행) to talk about current actions or activities. Make the present continuous tense like this:

be verb + verb −ing (am, is, are)

Use the words **now** or **right now** with the present continuous tense.

Q: What are you doing now? A: I am watching television now.
Q: What is Mark eating right now? A: He is eating a sandwich right now.
Q: Who is Tina meeting now? A: She is meeting her classmates now.
Q: What is the dog doing right now? A: It is sleeping right now.
Q: What are we studying now? A: We are studying English conversation now.
Q: Where are they going right now? A: They are going to a restaurant right now.

B *Look at the pictures. Then, complete the sentences.*

He's ____________________.

She's ____________________.

They're ____________________.

She's ____________________.

They're ____________________.

He's ____________________.

They're ____________________.

She's ____________________.

He's ____________________.

C Match the phrases to make complete sentences.

1. ______ The students are	A. catching the bank robber now.
2. ______ The doctor is	B. talking to my mother now.
3. ______ The policemen are	C. chasing the mouse now.
4. ______ The chef is	D. taking care of the patient now.
5. ______ My father is	E. lecturing to the students now.
6. ______ The teacher is	F. studying for a test right now.
7. ______ The cat is	G. going to the game now.
8. ______ The soccer player is	H. cooking dinner right now.

D Circle the mistakes. Then, write the correct sentences.

1. My brother is use his computer now. → ______
2. What am you doing now? → ______
3. We are meeting last night. → ______
4. Is where he going right now? → ______
5. I am practicing the piano now right. → ______
6. They are eat some cheesecake now. → ______
7. Is she does talking on the phone now? → ______
8. Mr. Kim reading a book right now. → ______

E Read the information below.

Answer yes/no questions in the present continuous tense two ways. First, give a short answer with "yes" or "no." Then, give more information.

Q: Are you reading a book now?
A: Yes, I am. I am reading my math textbook now.

Q: Is Sumi doing her homework now?
A: No, she is not. She is cleaning her room now.

Q: Are your friends going home now?
A: No, they aren't. They are going to the movie theater now.

Q: Are Nancy and Minho eating now?
A: Yes, they are. They are having pasta now.

5. Conversation 2 *The Future*

Sujin: When does your last class finish?
Nancy: It finishes at three o'clock.
Sujin: What are you doing after class?
Nancy: I'm going to the library.
Sujin: Okay. Well, what are you doing tomorrow?
Nancy: I don't have any plans. Why?
Sujin: I'm having dinner with Changhoon. Why don't you have dinner with us?
Nancy: Sure. That's a great idea.

Sujin: 마지막 수업이 언제 끝나니?
Nancy: 세 시에 끝나.
Sujin: 수업 끝나고 뭐할 건데?
Nancy: 도서관에 갈 거야.
Sujin: 그래. 내일은 뭐할 건데?
Nancy: 별일 없어. 왜?
Sujin: 창훈이랑 저녁 먹을 거야. 우리랑 같이 먹을래?
Nancy: 그래. 좋은 생각이야.

6. Let's Learn More 2

A *Read the information below.*

You can use the present continuous tense to talk about the future (미래). Just use future time words. Here are some future time words:

after class 수업 끝나고 **this evening** 오늘 저녁에 **tonight** 오늘 밤에
tomorrow 내일 **soon** 곧 **in a while** 얼마 있다가
this weekend 이번 주말에 **this Monday/Tuesday** 이번 월요일/화요일에
next Wednesday/Thursday 다음 수요일/목요일에
next week/month/year 다음 주/달/내년에
tomorrow morning/afternoon/evening/night 내일 아침/오후/저녁/밤에

Q: What are you doing after class? A: I am having lunch after class.
Q: What is Sumi doing tomorrow? A: She's studying her major tomorrow.
Q: Where are you going this weekend? A: I'm going to Gangnam this weekend.
Q: Who is Mark meeting this Friday? A: He is meeting his parents this Friday.
Q: What is Sujin doing next year? A: Sujin is graduating from school next year.

B *Read the conversation. Complete the sentences. Use the words in the box.*

weekend	going	Friday	leaving	taking	visiting

Changhoon: I'm really excited. I'm ________ to Seorak Mountain tomorrow.

Mark: Really? Why are you going there?

Changhoon: I'm ________ a trip with my friends.

Mark: That's great. I'm ________ my friend in Daegu this ________.

Changhoon: When are you ________?

Mark: I'm leaving this ________ night. I'm coming back to Seoul on Sunday.

C *Answer the questions.*

1. What are you doing after class? ________________
2. What are you doing this weekend? ________________
3. What are you eating tonight? ________________
4. What are you studying tomorrow? ________________
5. When is your family taking a trip? ________________
6. Who are you meeting tonight? ________________
7. Where is your brother/sister going tomorrow? ________________
8. How are your classmates going home tonight? ________________

D *Ask and answer questions using the present continuous tense. Write the answers.*

What are you doing ~?	Student 1	Student 2	Student 3
now			
after class			
tomorrow morning			
next week			
this vacation			
in the future			

7. Let's Learn About Culture

A Read the passage.

Every English sentence needs a subject and a verb. This is very important. However, many Korean sentences have no subject. For example, you can say this:

English	Korean
John: *What is Mark doing now?*	John: *Mark*는 지금 뭐하니?
Eric: *He is taking a test.*	Eric: 시험 보는 중이야.

In the Korean sentence, Eric does not use a subject. So, in English, that means, "Taking a test." In English, this is NOT a sentence. In English, you must ALWAYS use sentences. In addition, in American culture, people often use pronouns. These are words like **he**, **she**, **it**, **you**, **we**, and **they**. Pronouns are very important in English. With pronouns, you do NOT have to say a person's name again. Instead, you can use pronouns.

모든 영어 문장에는 주어와 동사가 있어야 한다. 영어에서 이것은 매우 중요하다. 그런데 많은 한국어 문장에는 주어가 없다. 예를 들어, 이렇게 말할 수 있는 것이다.

〈English〉	〈Korean〉
John: What is Mark doing now?	John: Mark는 지금 뭐 하니?
Eric: He is taking a test.	Eric: 시험 보는 중이야.

위의 한국어 대화에서 Eric은 말할 때 주어를 사용하지 않았다. 그렇게 되면 그 표현은 영어로는 그냥 "Taking a test." 밖에 안 되는데, 이것은 문장이 성립되지 않는다. 영어에서는 반드시 주어를 말해야 한다. 게다가 미국 문화에서는 주어를 대명사로 말한다. 대명사란 he, she, it, you, we, they 같은 것들이다. 영어에서는 대명사가 참 중요하다. 대명사를 쓰면 사람의 이름을 일일이 말할 필요가 없기 때문이다. 이름 대신 인칭대명사를 말하면 된다.

B Are these sentences (S) or not sentences (NS)? Write the answers.

1. ________ Talking to my friend.
2. ________ Are watching a movie now.
3. ________ Jason is having a party tonight.
4. ________ He's waiting for Sumi.
5. ________ I'm traveling to Busan tomorrow.
6. ________ Having lunch soon.

C *Change the nouns in the sentences to pronouns. Write the answers.*

1. Mark is going to church tomorrow. ______
2. Changhoon and John are taking a class now. ______
3. Nancy and I are going on a picnic. ______
4. Sujin is talking about her family. ______
5. The dog is playing with the toy. ______
6. David, Chris, and Jay are meeting tonight. ______

8. Use Your Knowledge

A *Look at the pictures. Then, answer the questions.*

1. What is Mark doing now? ______
2. What is Changhoon doing now? ______
3. What is Sumi doing now? ______
4. What is Nancy doing now? ______
5. What is Minho doing now? ______

1. What is Mr. Patterson doing right now? ______________________
2. What is Jason doing right now? ______________________
3. What is Tina doing right now? ______________________
4. What is David doing right now? ______________________
5. What is Mina doing right now? ______________________

Unit 3
My pencil is in my bag.

1. Vocabulary

fruit 과일
trashcan 쓰레기통
bowl 대접
pond 연못
location 위치
hill 언덕
thing 물건, ~것
It's my pleasure. 천만에요.
big problem 심각한 문제
What's the matter? 왜 그러세요?
late 늦은
anywhere 어디든지
across 건너서
backpack 배낭
clothes 옷, 의복
across from/opposite 길 건너편(에)
around the corner from 모퉁이를 돌아서
post office 우체국
real estate agency 부동산 중개소
landmark 경계표
rental car agency 렌터카 대여점
drugstore 약국

2. Let's Warm Up *Locations*

A *Look at the picture. Then, complete the sentences.*

1. The fruit is ___in___ the bowl.
2. The table is ________ the chairs.
3. The bowl is ________ the table.
4. The dog is ________ the table.
5. The book is ________ the bowl.
6. The book is ________ the table.

3. Conversation 1 *Locations of Things*

Listen to the conversation. Then, practice it with a partner.

Nancy: Oh, no! I have a big problem.
Sumi: What's the matter?
Nancy: I'm late for class.
And I can't find my book.
Sumi: Your book is under the desk.
Nancy: Oh, right. But where's my pencil?
Sumi: I don't see it anywhere.
Nancy: Aha! My pencil is in my bag.
Okay, I'm going to class now.
Sumi: See you later.

Nancy: 아, 이런! 심각한 문제가 생겼어.
Sumi: 왜 그래?
Nancy: 수업에 늦었는데 책을 못 찾겠어.
Sumi: 네 책은 책상 밑에 있어.
Nancy: 아, 그렇네.
그런데 연필은 어디 있지?
Sumi: 아무 데도 안 보이는데.
Nancy: 아하! 내 연필이 내 가방 안에 있네. 됐어, 이제 수업 들어가야지.
Sumi: 잘 다녀와.

4. Let's Learn More 1

A *Look at the pictures.*

on

in / inside

under / beneath

by / beside / next to

between

behind / in back of

in front of

across

Look at the picture. Then, answer the questions.

B

1. Where is the boy?

   The boy is on the bed.

2. Where is the desk?

3. Where is the computer?

4. Where are the books?

5. Where is the backpack?

6. Where are the clothes?

7. Where is the guitar?

8. Where is the trashcan?

9. Where is the picture?

10. Where is the bed?

C *Look at the picture. Write questions and answers with your partner. Then, practice asking and answering them.*

Question		Answer
1. the woman	*Where is the woman?*	*The woman is on the bench.*
2. the birds		
3. the cat		
4. the building		
5. the man		
6. the pond		
7. the girl		
8. the hill		

D *Think about your bedroom. Where is everything? Complete the sentences.*

1. My bed is ______.
2. My desk is ______.
3. My schoolbooks are ______.
4. My school bag is ______.
5. My clothes are ______.
6. My computer is ______.
7. My trashcan is ______.
8. My chair is ______.

5. Conversation 2 *Locations of Places*

Minho: Excuse me. Are you looking for something?
Mark: Yes, I am. I think I'm lost.
Minho: What are you looking for?
Mark: The buffet restaurant. Where is the buffet restaurant?
Minho: The buffet restaurant is next to the bank.
Mark: Oh, right. I can see it now. Thank you very much.
Minho: It's my pleasure. Have a nice day.
Mark: You, too.

Minho: 실례합니다. 어디를 찾고 계신가요?
Mark: 네. 제가 길을 잃은 것 같습니다.
Minho: 찾으시는 곳이 어딘데요?
Mark: 뷔페 식당이요. 뷔페 식당이 어디지요?
Minho: 뷔페 식당은 은행 옆에 있어요.
Mark: 아, 맞다. 이제 보이네요. 고맙습니다.
Minho: 천만에요. 안녕히 가세요.
Mark: 네.

6. Let's Learn More 2

A *Look at the pictures.*

across from / opposite

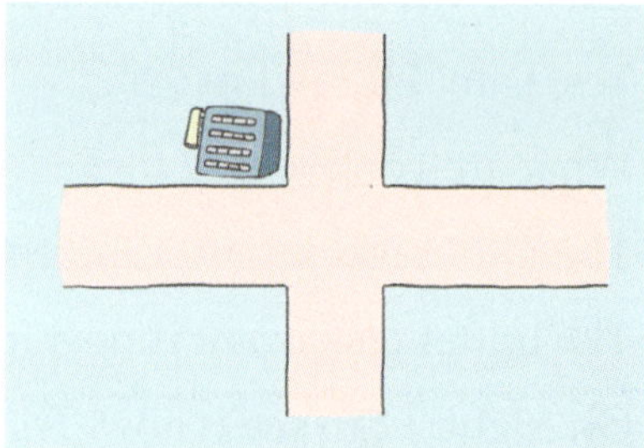

on the corner of

near / close to

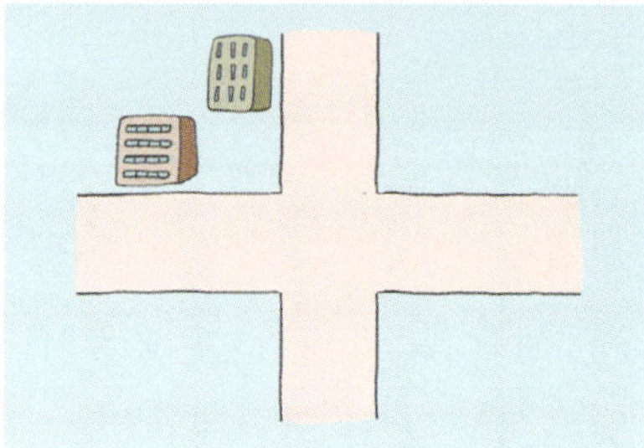

around the corner from

B *Look at the map. Then, answer the questions.*

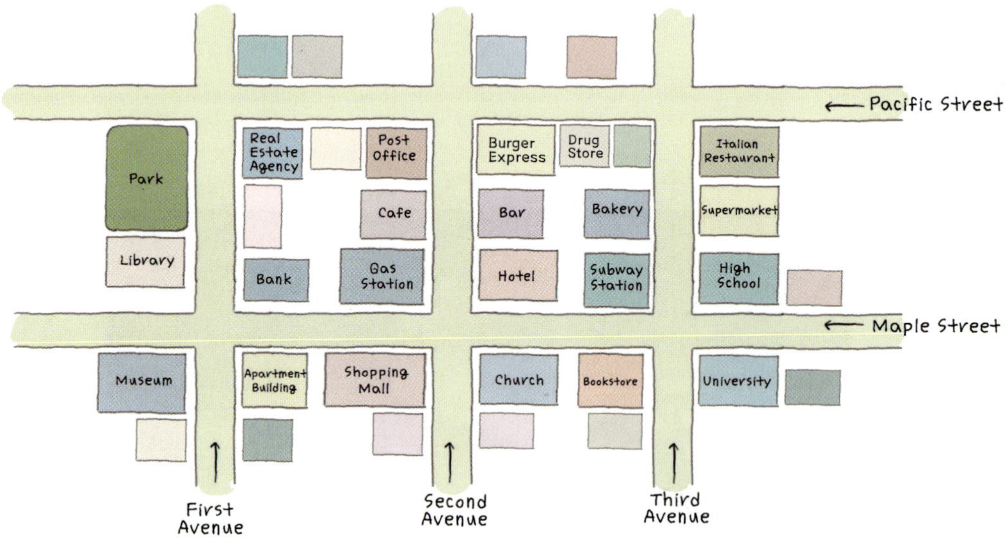

1. Where is the gas station? *It's on the corner of Maple Street and Second Avenue.*
2. Where is the cafe? ______
3. Where is the bookstore? ______
4. Where is the hotel? ______

C *Look at the map. Ask and answer questions with your partner.*

Question		Answer
1. church (bookstore)	*Where is the church?*	*The church is next to the bookstore.*
2. bar (Burger Express)		
3. high school (university)		
4. hotel (Maple Street)		

7. Let's Learn About Culture

A *Read the passage.*

In American culture, street names are very important. In Korean culture, street names are not very important. Many Americans give a street address to talk about a building's location. But Koreans usually mention landmarks. For example:

| American Style | | Korean Style |

A: *Where is the coffee shop?*

B: *It's at 120 Oak Street.*

| Korean Style |

A: *Where is the coffee shop?*

B: *It's next to the movie theater.*

In America, people only sometimes use landmarks. And in Korea, people almost never use addresses. However, you should know about both styles.

미국 문화에서는 길(거리) 이름이 매우 중요한 반면에, 한국 문화에서는 길 이름이 별로 중요하지 않다. 대다수의 미국인들은 건물의 위치를 말할 때 거리와 번지수를 얘기한다. 하지만 한국인들은 그 건물 가까운 곳에 있는 잘 알려진 곳이나 큰 건물을 말한다. 예를 들어,

| 미국식 |

A: 커피숍이 어디죠?

B: 오크 거리의 120번지입니다.

| 한국식 |

A: 커피숍이 어디죠?

B: 극장 옆에 있어요.

미국에서는 큰 건물이나 잘 알려진 곳을 얘기하는 경우가 드물다. 그리고 한국에서는 길을 가르쳐주면서 주소를 거의 사용하지 않는다. 그렇지만 양쪽 스타일은 모두 다 알고 있어야 한다.

B *Look at the map. Write the locations in the American style and the Korean style.*

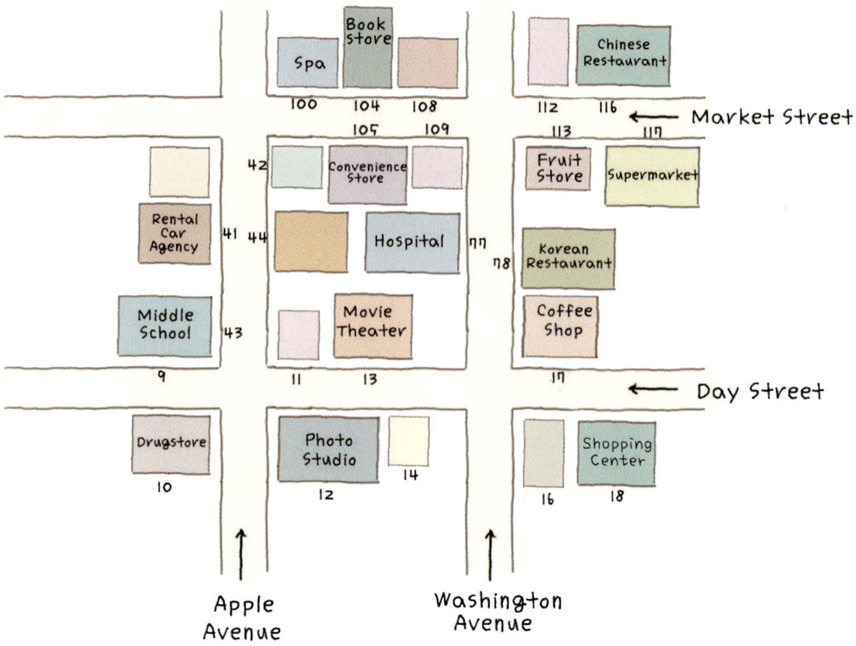

American Style

1. hospital — *The hospital is at 77 Washington Avenue.*
2. Chinese restaurant — ______________________
3. rental car agency — ______________________
4. drugstore — ______________________
5. coffee shop — ______________________
6. shopping center — ______________________

Korean Style

1. hospital — *The hospital is across from the Korean restaurant.*
2. coffee shop — ______________________
3. bookstore — ______________________
4. supermarket — ______________________
5. middle school — ______________________
6. movie theater — ______________________

8. Use Your Knowledge

A *Look at the picture.*

B *Write T (true) or F (false).*

1. ________ The puppy is under the bed.
2. ________ The computer is on the desk.
3. ________ All of the clothes are in the closet.
4. ________ The bag of food is in front of the girl.
5. ________ The CDs are on the floor.
6. ________ The sock is next to the desk.

C *Answer the questions.*

1. Where is the girl? ____________________
2. Where is the radio? ____________________
3. Where are the pencils? ____________________
4. Where are the shoes? ____________________
5. Where is the food? ____________________
6. Where are the books? ____________________

Unit 4

I watch television at five o'clock every day.

1. Vocabulary

bored 지루한, 따분한
every day 매일
documentary 다큐멘터리
love 사랑(하다)
noon 정오, 한낮
midnight 자정
PM 오후 (*post meridiem*)
AM 오전 (*ante meridiem*)
quarter 4분의 1, 15분, 25센트
past 지난
wake up 잠을 깨다
first/last class 첫/끝 수업
do one's homework 숙제를 하다
go to sleep 잠을 자다
stay home 집에 머물러 있다
go out 외출하다
exercise 운동(하다)
gym 헬스장
how often 얼마나 자주
visit 찾아가다
take the bus 버스를 타다
cook 음식을 만들다, 조리사
bar 술집, 감옥(창살)
Western food 서양 음식
exact 정확한
general 일반적인
begin 시작하다
arrive 도착하다

2. Let's Warm Up *Daily Schedule*

Write down your daily schedule. What do you do in the ________ ?

Morning:
Afternoon:
Evening:
Night:

3. Conversation 1 *Time*

Listen to the conversation. Then, practice it with a partner.

Jason: I'm bored. Let's do something.
Changhoon: What time is it?
Jason: It's four thirty. Why?
Changhoon: I watch television at five o'clock every day.
Jason: Really? What program do you watch?
Changhoon: It's a documentary. I love that program.
Jason: What time do you finish watching the program?
Changhoon: At six. Then, I have dinner around six fifteen.

Jason: 심심하다. 뭐 좀 하자.
Changhoon: 지금 몇 시니?
Jason: 네 시 반이야. 왜?
Changhoon: 난 매일 다섯 시에 텔레비전을 보거든.
Jason: 그래? 어떤 프로그램을 보는데?
Changhoon: 다큐멘터리야. 난 그 프로그램을 좋아해.
Jason: 그 프로그램이 몇 시에 끝나니?
Changhoon: 여섯 시. 그리고 나서 난 여섯 시 십오 분쯤에 저녁을 먹어.

4. Let's Learn More 1

A *Look at the different ways to tell time. Practice the sentences with your partner.*

Q: What time is it? A: It's ______________.

twelve PM / twelve AM
noon / midnight

two fifteen
a quarter after / past two
two fifteen in the afternoon

seven thirty
half past seven

ten forty-five
ten forty-five at night
a quarter to eleven

one-oh five
five past / after one

four fifty
ten to five

B *What time is it? Look at the clocks. Then, write the correct times.*

It's five o'clock/It's five PM.

____

____

____

____

____

C *Complete the chart about your daily schedule. Then, talk to your partner.*

What do you do at ~?

8:00 AM:	4:00 PM:
10:00 AM:	6:00 PM:
12:00 PM:	9:00 PM:
1:00 PM:	1:00 AM:

D *Answer the questions.*

1. What time do you wake up? ______________________
2. What time do you go to school? ______________________
3. What time do you have your first class? ______________________
4. What time do you have your last class? ______________________
5. When do you have dinner? ______________________
6. When do you go home? ______________________
7. When do you do your homework? ______________________
8. When do you go to sleep? ______________________

E *Complete the sentences.*

1. I ______________________ in the morning.
2. I ______________________ in the afternoon.
3. I ______________________ in the evening.
4. I ______________________ at night.
5. I ______________________ on the weekend.
6. I ______________________ every day.

5. Conversation 2 *Regular Activities*

Sujin: What do you usually do on the weekend?
Tina: I usually go shopping on the weekend.
What about you?
Sujin: I sometimes stay home.
Tina: Don't you ever go out?
Sujin: Oh, of course.
I often exercise at the gym.
Tina: How often do you exercise?
Sujin: I exercise twice a week.

Sujin: 너 주말에는 보통 뭐하니?
Tina: 난 주말에 보통 쇼핑하러 가.
너는?
Sujin: 난 이따금 집에 있어.
Tina: 밖에는 안 나가니?
Sujin: 아, 물론 나가지.
종종 헬스장에 가서 운동을 해.
Tina: 운동을 얼마나 자주 하는데?
Sujin: 일주일에 두 번 정도 해.

6. Let's Learn More 2

A *Read the information below.*

Yon can use adverbs (부사) to talk about how often you do something. There are many adverbs. Some common adverbs are **always**, **usually**, **often**, **sometimes**, and **never**. Use them in sentences like this:

subject (주어)	+	adverb (부사)	+	verb (동사)	+	object (목적어)

I always do my homework.
Mary usually calls her parents.
Isaac often checks his email.
We sometimes listen to music.
Good students never forget their books.

B *Answer the questions.*

1. What do you usually do after school? *I often have dinner after school.*
2. Where do you usually go in the morning? ____________________
3. What do you usually eat? ____________________
4. Who do you usually talk to on the phone? ____________________
5. How often do you meet your friends? ____________________
6. How often do you play computer games? ____________________
7. How often do you do your homework? ____________________
8. How often do you drink soju? ____________________

C *Read the information below.*

There are a lot of ways to answer the question, "How often do you ~?" You can use many expressions. Use each of these expressions at the end of a sentence:

once a day/one time a day 하루에 한 번
as often as possible 가능한 한 자주
twice a week/two times a week 일주일에 두 번
every day 매일
three times a month 한 달에 세 번
every week/month/year 매주/달/년
a lot 많이
all the time 항상

D *Write the answers. Then, ask and answer the questions with your partner.*

1. How often do you eat? ____________________
2. How often do you use social media? ____________________
3. How often do you watch TV? ____________________
4. How often do you cook? ____________________
5. How often do you go to school? ____________________
6. How often do you exercise? ____________________
7. How often do you take a trip? ____________________

7. Let's Learn About Culture

A *Read the passage.*

In American culture, time is very important. Many Americans want to know the exact time something will happen. In Korean culture, people often talk about "Korean time." Many Koreans are not exact about time. Because time is very important in America, there are many words to use for time. For example:

> *The movie begins at seven thirty* ***on the dot****.*
> *The meeting starts* ***right at*** *two.*

You can also use **exactly**, **precisely**, and **sharp**.
Those expressions are for an exact period of time. However, sometimes you may not be sure of the exact time. You want to talk about a general time. Then, you can use these expressions:

> *We are meeting* ***around*** *eight o'clock.*
> *John is coming* ***at about*** *noon.*

미국 문화에서는 시간이 매우 중요하다. 미국 사람들은 대부분 어떤 일이 정확히 언제 일어나는지 알고 싶어한다. 한국 문화에서는 사람들이 흔히 "코리아 타임"이라는 말을 많이 한다. 한국 사람들은 대부분 시간에 관하여 정확하지 않은 편이다. 미국에서는 시간이 매우 중요하기 때문에 시간에 관한 중요한 표현들이 많이 있다. 예를 들어,

> 영화는 7시 반에 **정확히(on the dot)** 시작한다.
> 회의는 2시에 **바로(right)** 시작된다.

또한 exactly, precisely 및 sharp도 사용할 수 있다.
위의 표현들은 정확한 시각을 나타내는 것들이지만 때로는 정확한 시간을 알 수가 없는 경우도 있다. 그럴 때는 일반적인 시간을 말해야 한다. 그런 경우에 다음과 같은 표현을 사용하면 된다.

> 우리는 **8시쯤(around)**에 만나기로 했어요.
> 존은 **정오경(at about)**에 올 거야.

B *Are these sentences about exact (E) times or general (G) times?*

1. __________ Come to my house at three o'clock sharp.
2. __________ Class always begins precisely at five thirty.
3. __________ I'm going to arrive around seven.

4. ____________ Let's meet at about one.
5. ____________ The game starts right at nine.
6. ____________ Mina eats lunch exactly at noon.

8. Use Your Knowledge

A *Look at the pictures.*

B *How often do you do the activities above? Complete the questions and answers. Then, practice them with your partner.*

1. *How often do you play soccer?* ____________ *I sometimes play soccer.* ____________
2. *How often do you* ____________ ____________
3. ____________ ____________
4. ____________ ____________
5. ____________ ____________
6. ____________ ____________
7. ____________ ____________
8. ____________ ____________

Unit 5

There are five people in my family.

1. Vocabulary

article 글, 품목, 신문기사	**Wow.** 우와~
office worker 회사원	**banker** 은행 직원, 은행가
Cool. 좋다.	**try** 시도하다
grow crops 농작물을 재배하다	**carry** 운반하다
raise animals 동물을 기르다	**stationery store** 문구점
work with ~ ~와 함께 일하다	**join** 함께 하다
secretary 비서	**military** 군대의, 육군의
chemist 화학자	**travel agent** 여행사 직원
protect 보호하다	**manager** 매니저, 팀장, 책임자
citizen 시민	**envy** 부러워하다
That sounds like ~ 그 말은 듣고 보니 ~하다.	**housewife** 가정주부
I want to become ~ 나는 ~이 되고 싶다.	**real estate agency** 부동산 중개소
author 작가, 저자	**personal** 개인적인

2. Let's Warm Up *Family Members*

Do you know these words? What do they mean?

mother	grandfather	niece
father	aunt	grandson
sister	uncle	granddaughter
brother	cousin	mother-in-law
grandmother	nephew	father-in-law

3. Conversation 1 *Family Members*

Listen to the conversation. Then, practice it with a partner.

Sumi: How many people are in your family, Mark?
Mark: There are six people in my family.
Sumi: Who are they?
Mark: My mother, father, older sister, two younger brothers, and me.
Sumi: You have a big family. What does your father do?
Mark: He's a banker. And my mother is a teacher.
Sumi: Cool. My father has a restaurant. And my mother works at a hospital.

Sumi: 마크야, 너희 가족은 모두 몇 명이니?
Mark: 우리 가족은 모두 여섯 명이야.
Sumi: 누구 누군데?
Mark: 엄마, 아빠, 누나, 남동생 둘, 나.
Sumi: 식구 많네. 아버지는 뭐하시니?
Mark: 은행에서 일하셔. 엄마는 선생님이시고.
Sumi: 좋구나. 우리 아빠는 음식점을 경영하셔. 엄마는 병원에서 일하시고.

4. Let's Learn More 1

A *Answer the questions.*

1. How many people are in your family? ______________________
2. How many brothers do you have? ______________________
3. How many sisters do you have? ______________________
4. What is your father's name? ______________________
5. What is your mother's name? ______________________
6. Who is your favorite family member? ______________________
7. What does your brother / sister do? ______________________

B Read the information below.

In the present simple tense, sometimes you must change the ending of the verb. When the subject is **he**, **she**, or **it**, you must add **-s**, **-es**, or **-ies** to the verb. Look at the examples:

play → plays
eat → eats
work → works
*** *have → has*

go → goes
do → does
watch → watches

study → studies
try → tries
carry → carries

C Circle the mistakes. Then, write the correct sentences.

1. I likes Korean food very much. ______________________
2. My brother own a stationery store. ______________________
3. Does she likes her major? ______________________
4. Sumi teach elementary school students. ______________________
5. Jason live near his parents. ______________________
6. What do Changhoon eat after work? ______________________

D Ask and answer questions about your family with your partners. Write the answers.

What does your ~ do?	Student 1	Student 2	Student 3
father			
mother			
sister			
brother			
best friend			

5. Conversation 2 *Jobs*

Changhoon: I am joining the military soon.
Nancy: Really? What does a Korean soldier do?
Changhoon: A soldier protects the citizens of the country.
Nancy: That sounds like a good job.
Changhoon: Yeah, but it's difficult. What do you want to do in the future?
Nancy: I want to become an author.
Changhoon: What does an author do?
Nancy: An author writes books and articles.

Changhoon: 나 곧 군대 가.
Nancy: 그래? 한국 군인들은 무슨 일을 하니?
Changhoon: 군인은 국민을 보호하지.
Nancy: 좋은 일을 하는 것 같구나.
Changhoon: 응, 그런데 힘들어. 넌 앞으로 어떤 일을 하고 싶니?
Nancy: 난 작가가 되고 싶어.
Changhoon: 작가는 어떤 일을 하는데?
Nancy: 작가는 책과 글을 쓰지.

6. Let's Learn More 2

A *Match the phrases to make complete sentences.*

1. A salesman	A. grows crops and raises animals.
2. An office worker	B. helps sick people get better.
3. A doctor	C. works at a company or business.
4. A tour guide	D. sells items to customers.
5. A farmer	E. works with computers.
6. A computer programmer	F. takes tourists to different places.

B *Answer the questions.*

1. What does a secretary do? ______________________
2. What does a teacher do? ______________________
3. What does a chemist do? ______________________
4. What does a chef do? ______________________
5. What does a police officer do? ______________________
6. What does a firefighter do? ______________________
7. What does an athlete do? ______________________
8. What does a travel agent do? ______________________

C *Read the conversation. Complete the sentences. Use the words in the box.*

does	businesswoman	salesman	student	department

Sujin: Do you have a job now, Minho?

Minho: No, I don't. I'm a ____________ at a university. How about you?

Sujin: I don't have a job either. But my best friend is a ____________. She works for a big company.

Minho: What ____________ she do there?

Sujin: She is a manager at her company. And my brother is a ____________. He works at a large ____________ store.

Minho: They both have good jobs. I envy them.

D *Read the information below.*

Make negatives in the present simple tense with **not**. Use them in sentences like this:

subject + do/does + not + verb + object
(doesn't)

I do not have a car.
Tina does not know his name.
We do not understand the question.

You do not remember the answer.
Changhoon does not have any money.
They do not like sports.

E Change the following sentences into negative ones.

1. Mr. Kim lives in Seoul. → *Mr. Kim does not live in Seoul.*
2. We like to watch this television program. → ______________________
3. Nancy works at a small company. → ______________________
4. I study math every day. → ______________________
5. The students like their majors very much. → ______________________
6. Sumi has one brother and two sisters. → ______________________
7. My mother is a housewife. → ______________________
8. Greg owns a real estate agency. → ______________________

F Read the information below.

In Korea, age is very important. So Koreans often ask about age. You can ask about age like this:

Q: How old are you?
A: I am twenty years old.

Q: How old is he/she?
A: He/She is twenty-five.

Sometimes, you might not know a person's age. So you can use these descriptions:

Age		Expression
13~19	=	in one's teens
20~29	=	in one's twenties
30~39	=	in one's thirties
40~49	=	in one's forties
50~59	=	in one's fifties
60~69	=	in one's sixties
70~79	=	in one's seventies
80~89	=	in one's eighties
90~99	=	in one's nineties

7. Let's Learn About Culture

A *Read the passage.*

In both Korean and American culture, people like talking about their families. However, in American culture, some questions are very bad. You should NOT ask these questions in English:

Why don't you have a baby?
Why are you divorced? (Why are your parents divorced?)
What's your salary?

Americans think these are very personal questions. you may be curious... BUT don't ask personal questions. They are very rude in English. In addition, age is not important to many Americans. They often do not know other people's ages. And they almost never ask. Some good questions to ask about families are:

What does your mother/father do?
Where does your family live?
How many brothers/sisters do you have?

한국과 미국 문화 모두 가족에 대해서 얘기하는 것을 좋아한다. 그런데 미국 문화에서는 다음과 같은 질문을 하면 안 된다.

당신은 왜 아이가 없어요?
당신은 왜 이혼했나요? (너희 부모님은 왜 이혼하셨니?)
당신은 월급이 얼마예요?

미국인들은 위와 같은 것들이 너무 개인적인 질문이라고 생각한다. 그러므로 궁금하더라도 절대로 개인적인 질문을 해서는 안 된다. 영어에서는 상당한 실례이기 때문이다. 게다가 나이는 미국 사람들 대부분에게 그리 중요한 것이 아니다. 그들은 다른 사람들의 나이를 모르고 지내는 경우가 많다. 그리고 그들은 나이를 거의 묻지 않는다. 가족에 대해서 물을 수 있는 좋은 질문들은 다음과 같다.

너희 어머니/아버지는 뭐하시니?
너희 가족은 어디에 사니?
너는 형제/자매가 몇 명이니?

B *Are these questions polite (P) or impolite (I) in American culture? Write the answers.*

1. ________ How much money does your brother make?
2. ________ What does your sister do?
3. ________ When will you get married?
4. ________ Where does your grandmother live?
5. ________ Why is your brother not married?
6. ________ Why is your uncle divorced?
7. ________ How many cousins do you have?
8. ________ When are you and your wife having a baby?

8. Use Your Knowledge

A *Look at the picture. Then, answer the questions.*

1. What does Mr. Johnson do? ________________
2. What does Mrs. Johnson do? ________________
3. What does Brian Johnson do? ________________
4. What does Lisa Johnson do? ________________

B *Look at the picture. Then, write the questions and answers.*

1. *What does Mr. Park do?* ____________________
2. ____________________ ____________________
3. ____________________ ____________________
4. ____________________ ____________________

Unit 6
I can play the piano and sing.

1. Vocabulary

skill 기술
ability 능력
repair 수리하다
move 움직이다, 이사하다
chase 쫓다
bake 굽다
math problem 수학 문제
type 타입, 스타일, 타자치다
make friends with ~ ~와 사귀다
create 창조하다, 창안하다
best friend 제일 친한 친구
modest 겸손한
I don't know how. 어떻게 하는지 모른다.
foreign language 외국어
use a computer 컴퓨터를 사용하다
play the piano 피아노를 연주하다
Chinese characters 한자
tell a joke 농담하다
be good at ~ ~을 잘하다
be bad at ~ ~을 잘못하다
How well can you ~? 너는 ~을 얼마나 잘하니?
Do you know how to ~? ~을 어떻게 하는지 아니?
take care of 돌보다, 처리하다

2. Let's Warm Up *Skills and Abilities*

What can you do?

Can you ~?

1. sing
2. dance
3. speak a foreign language
4. drive a car
5. swim
6. use a computer
7. cook
8. paint
9. play the piano
10. ride a bicycle
11. play a sport
12. read Chinese characters

3. Conversation 1 *Can*

Listen to the conversation. Then, practice it with a partner.

Sujin: What are you doing this weekend, Nancy?
Nancy: I'm going swimming. Can you swim?
Sujin: No, I can't. But I want to learn.
Nancy: I can teach you. It's really easy.
Sujin: That's great. What else can you do?
Nancy: Hmm. I can play the piano and sing.
Sujin: So can I. I can also dance.
Nancy: Wow. You can do many different things.

Sujin: 낸시야, 이번 주말에 뭐하니?
Nancy: 수영하러 가. 너 수영할 줄 아니?
Sujin: 아니. 그래도 배우고 싶어.
Nancy: 내가 가르쳐줄게. 정말 쉬워.
Sujin: 잘됐다. 그거 말고 넌 뭘 할 수 있니?
Nancy: 흠. 난 피아노도 치고 노래도 할 수 있어.
Sujin: 나도 그래. 난 춤도 출 수 있다.
Nancy: 우와. 넌 할 줄 아는 게 많구나.

4. Let's Learn More 1

A *Read the information below.*

Use **can** and **cannot** to talk about people's skills and abilities. Use them in sentences like this:

subject + can/cannot + verb + object

I can play the violin.
Jason can speak German.
Sujin can in-line skate.

Nancy cannot drive a bus.
Minho cannot play ice hockey.
They cannot bake cookies.

B *What are your skills and abilities?*

나의 두뇌 능력	나의 육체적 능력
1. *I can do math problems.*	1. *I can run fast.*
2.	2.
3.	3.
4.	4.
5.	5.
6.	6.
7.	7.
8.	8.
9.	9.
10.	10.
나의 창의적 능력	**기타 능력**
1. *I can dance.*	1. *I can make friends with people.*
2.	2.
3.	3.
4.	4.
5.	5.
6.	6.
7.	7.
8.	8.
9.	9.
10.	10.

C *Answer the questions.*

1. Can you type? ______________________
2. Can you understand Japanese? ______________________
3. Can you create your own webpage? ______________________
4. Can you run for ten minutes? ______________________
5. Can your best friend speak English? ______________________
6. Can your mother drive a car? ______________________
7. Can your father play computer games? ______________________
8. Can your brother / sister cook? ______________________

D *Read the information below. Then answer the questions.*

Give two answers to questions starting with "can." First, answer "yes" or "no." Then, give more information. Look at the following questions and answers.

Q: Can you speak a foreign language. A: Yes, I can. I can speak English.
Q: Can you cook? A: Yes, I can. I can cook Korean and Italian food.
Q: Can you paint? A: No, I can't. I don't know how.
Q: Can you drive a bus? A: No, I can't. But I can drive a car.

1. Can you swim? ______________________
2. Can you ride a bicycle? ______________________
3. Can you repair a computer? ______________________
4. Can you play American football? ______________________
5. Can you sing? ______________________
6. Can you play the trumpet? ______________________

E Circle the correct answers.

1. An elephant (can / cannot) fly.
2. A shark (can / cannot) swim.
3. A snake (can / cannot) walk.
4. A snail (can / cannot) move very quickly.
5. A dog (can / cannot) be a good friend.
6. A cat (can / cannot) chase mice.

F *Ask your partners about their skills and abilities. Write the answers.*

Can you ~?	Student 1	Student 2	Student 3
play a sport			
speak two languages			
cook			
use a computer			
tell a good joke			
draw pictures			

5. Conversation 2 *Regular Activities*

Mark: Chinese characters are really difficult. I can't learn them.
Changhoon: Yes, you can. I know you can do it.
Mark: Thanks. Can you read Chinese characters?
Changhoon: Yes, I can. But I can't read them well.
Mark: Do you know any foreign languages?
Changhoon: I can speak German very well.
Mark: I can't do that. But I can speak a little French.
Changhoon: I can't speak French at all.

Mark: 한자는 너무 어려워. 나 못 배울 것 같아.
Changhoon: 아니야, 배울 수 있어. 난 네가 할 수 있다는 걸 알아.
Mark: 고마워. 너는 한자 읽을 줄 아니?
Changhoon: 응. 그런데 잘 읽지는 못해.
Mark: 또 다른 외국어 아는 것 있니?
Changhoon: 난 독일어를 참 잘해.
Mark: 난 못해. 하지만 난 프랑스어를 좀 하지.
Changhoon: 난 프랑스어 전혀 못해.

6. Let's Learn More 2

A *Read the information below.*

You probably have many different skills and abilities. But you do not do them all equally as well. Talk about your abilities like this:

Q: Can you speak Chinese well? A: Yes, I can. I am very good at Chinese.
Q: Can you cook well? A: No, I can't. I can only cook a little.

Positive Expressions

I can drive a car really well.

I can play baseball pretty well.

I am good at cooking.

I am great at computer games.

Negative Expressions

I can't drive a car very well.

I can't play baseball at all.

I am bad at cooking.

I am terrible at computer games.

B *Answer the questions.*

1. Can you dance well? ______________________
2. Can you write well? ______________________
3. Can you drive a car well? ______________________
4. Can you cook well? ______________________
5. How well can you make friends? ______________________
6. How well can you ice skate? ______________________

C Read the information below.

Use "Do you know ~?" to ask about a person's skills, abilities, or knowledge. Ask about them like this:

Do you know + noun Do you know how to + verb

**** The noun is usually plural.*

Q: Do you know Spanish?
A: Yes, I do. I can speak Spanish.

Q: Do you know the guitar?
A: No, I don't. I can't play the guitar.

Q: Do you know how to ride a bike?
A: Yes, I do. I can ride a bike very well.

Q: Do you know how to play soccer?
A: No, I don't. I can't play soccer at all.

D *Answer the questions. Then, practice them with your partner.*

1. Do you know French? *No, I don't. I can't speak any French.*
2. Do you know engineering? ______________________
3. Do you know the piano? ______________________
4. Do you know how to ski? ______________________
5. Do you know how to go to Busan? ______________________
6. Do you know how to take care of a dog? ______________________
7. Do you know how to fly an airplane? ______________________
8. Do you know how to surf the Internet? ______________________

7. Let's Learn About Culture

A *Read the passage.*

Koreans are often very modest about their skills and abilities. They might know something very well. BUT... They might say, "I can't do it well," or, "I'm not very good at it." They can do it, but they are being modest. However, many Americans will say, "I can do it well," or, "I'm very good at it." This is an important cultural difference. This is very important for job interviews. There are many foreign companies in Korean. At a job interview at a foreign company, you should NOT be modest. Say, "I'm good at it," or, "I can do it pretty well." This should help you in future job interviews.

한국인들은 자신의 기술과 능력에 대해서 아주 겸손한 경우가 많다. 어떤 것을 아주 잘 알고 있지만 "저 그거 잘 못해요." 또는 "그것에 별 재주가 없어요."라고 말한다. 그것을 할 수 있지만 겸손한 것이다. 그러나 미국인들이라면 "저 그거 잘해요." 또는 "그것에 소질이 있습니다."라고 말할 것이다. 이것은 중요한 문화 차이다. 한국에는 외국 회사가 많이 있다. 외국 회사에서 취업 면접을 하는 경우라면 겸손해서는 안 된다. "제가 그것을 잘합니다." 아니면 "제가 그것에 소질이 있습니다."라고 말하라. 그렇게 하면 취업 면접에서 도움이 될 것이다.

B *Is the person being modest (M) or honest (H)? Write the answers.*

1. ______ A student can speak English, Korean, Chinese, and French. She says, "I cannot speak foreign languages very well."
2. ______ A student got a 95 on an exam in his major. He says, "I am just okay at my major."
3. ______ A student can play the piano, violin, and flute. She says, "I can play musical instruments very well."
4. ______ A student cooks delicious dinners for his family every night. He says, "I am poor at cooking."
5. ______ A student cannot play any sports well. He says, "I'm terrible at sports."
6. ______ A student helps other people make their own websites. She says, "I'm pretty good at using computers."

8. Use Your Knowledge

A *Look at the picture. Then, answer the questions.*

What can Minho do?

1. *Minho can play the guitar.*
2. ______
3. ______
4. ______
5. ______
6. ______
7. ______
8. ______

What can Nancy do?

1. *Nancy can read Japanese.*
2. ______
3. ______
4. ______
5. ______
6. ______
7. ______
8. ______

Unit 7

Did you have a good weekend?

1. Vocabulary

past 지난	**forget** 잊다
action 행동	**choose** 선택하다
specific 구체적인	**seem** ~인 듯하다
order 주문하다, 명령하다, 질서	**Cool.** 좋다
Thanks for saying that. 그렇게 말해줘서 고마워.	**past simple tense** 단순 과거시제
couple 둘, 부부	**stop** 멈추다
greet 인사하다	**wear** 입다
pattern 무늬, 패턴	**subject** 주제, 과목, 주어
memorize 외우다	**time expression** 시간 표현
leave 떠나다, 뒤에 남기다	**report** 보고하다, 보고서
enter 들어가다	**everyone** 모든 사람들
ask 묻다, 부탁하다	**for ~ years** ~년 동안
become ~이 되다	**take a test** 시험을 치다
arrive 도착하다	**check email** 이메일을 확인하다

2. Let's Warm Up *Last Week's Activities*

What did you do last week? Write your activities for each day.

Monday: Tuesday:
Wednesday: Thursday:
Friday: Saturday:
Sunday:

3. Conversation 1 *The Past Simple Tense*

Listen to the conversation. Then, practice it with a partner.

Tina: Did you have a good weekend, Sumi?

Sumi: Yes, I did. I watched a movie last weekend.

Tina: Who did you see it with?

Sumi: I saw it with my boyfriend.

Tina: I know your boyfriend. I met him last week, right?

Sumi: Yes, you did. Did you like him?

Tina: Yeah. He seemed very nice.

Sumi: Thanks for saying that.

Tina: 수미야, 주말 잘 보냈니?

Sumi: 응. 지난 주말에 영화봤어.

Tina: 누구와 함께 봤는데?

Sumi: 내 남자친구랑 봤어.

Tina: 나 너의 남자친구 알아. 내가 지난주에 만났었지, 그렇지?

Sumi: 응. 마음에 들었니?

Tina: 그래. 아주 괜찮아 보이더라.

Sumi: 그렇게 말해줘서 고마워.

4. Let's Learn More 1

A Read the information below.

Use the past simple tense to talk about actions or activities in the past.
English has regular verbs (규칙동사) and irregular verbs (불규칙동사). For regular verbs, form the past simple tense like this:

> verb + –d/–ed/–ied

Look at the following verbs:

play → played
stop → stopped
study → studied
greet → greeted
work → worked
dance → danced

For irregular verbs, there is NO pattern. Every verb has a different past tense form. You must memorize these. Here are some irregular verbs and their past tense forms:

come → came
do → did
eat → ate
find → found
give → gave
know → knew
leave → left
make → made
meet → met
read → read
speak → spoke
teach → taught

B Write the past tense forms of the verbs.

1. see ______________
2. think ______________
3. love ______________
4. enter ______________
5. take ______________
6. watch ______________
7. ask ______________
8. go ______________
9. become ______________
10. talk ______________
11. drink ______________
12. start ______________
13. arrive ______________
14. begin ______________
15. forget ______________
16. choose ______________

C *Answer the questions.*

1. What did you do yesterday? ______________________
2. What did you do this morning? ______________________
3. What did you eat today? ______________________
4. How did you come to school today? ______________________
5. Where did your father go last night? ______________________
6. Who did your mother call yesterday? ______________________
7. When did your friends meet you? ______________________
8. When did your classmate take a test? ______________________

5. Conversation 2 *Asking about Specific Activities*

Jason: Did you order some food?
Minho: Yes, I called the restaurant ten minutes ago.
Jason: Great. What food did you order?
Minho: I ordered a pepperoni pizza.
Jason: Cool. Pizza is my favorite food.
Minho: Oh, did you reserve movie tickets? What kind of movie are we seeing?
Jason: Yes, I did. I reserved tickets for an action movie.

Jason: 음식 주문했니?
Minho: 응, 10분 전에 음식점에 전화했어.
Jason: 좋았어. 어떤 음식을 시켰니?
Minho: 페퍼로니 피자를 한 판 샀어.
Jason: 좋았어. 피자는 내가 제일 좋아하는 음식이야.
Minho: 아, 너 영화 티켓 예매했니? 우리 어떤 영화 볼 거니?
Jason: 응, 했어. 액션 영화 티켓을 예매했지.

6. Let's Learn More 2

A Read the information below.

Use "What + noun" to ask about specific activities. Look at the examples:

Q: What food did you order? A: I ordered a pizza.
Q: What music did you listen to? A: I listened to some pop songs.
Q: What clothes did you wear? A: I wore a suit.
Q: What bus did you take? A: I took the number 99 bus.

B Make questions with the words below. Then, answer them with your partner.

Q: What subject did you study yesterday?
A: I studied English yesterday

1. subject / study / yesterday Q: A:	2. food / cook / last night Q: A:
3. movie / watch / last week Q: A:	4. time / wake up / this morning Q: A:
5. computer game / play / in the past Q: A:	6. TV program / see / on Friday night Q: A:
7. book / read / last weekend Q: A:	8. class / attend / at 11:00 Q: A:

C *Read the information below. Then, answer the questions.*

Time expressions are very important for the past tense. You should always use time expressions. Here are some of them:

yesterday 어제
last night 간밤에
yesterday morning/afternoon/evening 어제 아침/오후/저녁
last week/month/year 지난 주/달/작년
last Monday 지난 월요일
5 minutes ago 5분 전에
2 days ago 이틀 전에
3 months ago 석 달 전에
a while ago 좀 전에
in the past 예전에

D *Ask and answer questions about the past with your partners. Write the answers.*

What did you do ~?	Student 1	Student 2	Student 3
yesterday			
last weekend			
4 hours ago			
this morning			
at 10 last night			
last summer			

E *Circle the mistakes. Then, write the correct sentences.*

1. Minsu ate breakfast tomorrow. → ______________________
2. I did watched a movie yesterday. → ______________________
3. Our teacher not give us homework. → ______________________
4. Changhoon went home in five o'clock. → ______________________
5. They writed a report in their class. → ______________________
6. What did you read book last weekend? → ______________________

F Complete the sentences.

1. My mother ______________________________ yesterday.
2. My father ______________________________ two days ago.
3. My best friend ______________________________ last night.
4. My friend and I ______________________________ last weekend.
5. My brother / sister ______________________________ two weeks ago.
6. I ______________________________ last vacation.

7. Let's Learn About Culture

A Read the passage.

You should always use time words in English. Americans like to be very specific about time. So they often use times words. This is true for the past, present, and future. For example, you might say, "I went to school." But there is no time expression. When did you go to school? Today? Yesterday? Two days ago? Last week? In addition, you might say, "I'm going shopping." But there is no time expression here either. When are you going shopping? Now? In 5 minutes? Tonight? Tomorrow? Use time expressions, and your English will improve very much. Then, people will understand you much, much better.

영어에서는 항상 시간 표현을 사용한다. 미국 사람들은 구체적인 시간을 좋아한다. 그래서 시간 표현을 자주 사용하는데, 시간 표현에는 과거, 현재, 미래에 관한 것들이 있다. 예를 들어 "나는 학교에 갔다."라고 말하게 되면 여기에는 시간 표현이 들어 있지 않다. 도대체 언제 학교에 갔었다는 말인가? 오늘? 어제? 그저께? 지난주에? 또 "나는 쇼핑하러 갈 거야." 라고 말할 수도 있는데 여기도 시간 표현이 없다. 언제 쇼핑하러 갈 것인가? 지금? 5분 후에? 오늘 저녁에? 내일? 시간 표현을 사용하자. 그러면 여러분의 영어가 훨씬 향상될 것이다. 게다가 사람들이 여러분의 영어를 훨씬 더 잘 알아들을 것이다.

B Use time expressions to complete the sentences.

1. I took the bus to school ______________________________.
2. I ate breakfast ______________________________.
3. I played computer games ______________________________.
4. I did my homework ______________________________.

5. I am studying English ______________________________.
6. I am going home ______________________________.
7. I am taking a test ______________________________.
8. I am checking my email ______________________________.

8. Use Your Knowledge

A *Look at the pictures.*

B *Answer the questions. Then, practice them with your partner.*

1. What did Sumi do this morning? *Sumi drove her car this morning.*
2. What did Nancy do last night? ______________________________
3. What did Jason do last Friday? ______________________________
4. What did Minho do at 6:00 PM? ______________________________
5. What did Mark do last weekend? ______________________________
6. What did Changhoon do at 9 AM? ______________________________
7. What did Sujin do on Tuesday morning? ______________________________
8. What did Tina do 10 minutes ago? ______________________________

Unit 8
What's wrong with you?

1. Vocabulary

body part 신체 부위	**sickness** 병, 아픔, 통증
ache/pain 병, 통증	**knee** 무릎
You look ~ 너는 ~해 보인다.	**symptom** 증상
terrible 끔찍한	**forehead** 이마
awful 끔찍한, 굉장한	**move** 움직이다
fever 열	**or** 또는
sore throat 부어서 아픈 목	**but** 그러나, 그래도
You should ~ 너는 ~하는 게 좋다.	**stay** 머무르다
conjunction 접속사, 결합	**cough** 기침(하다)
sore 쑤시고 아픈	**earache** 귀앓이
apology 사과하다	**flu** 독감 (influenza의 준말)
insomnia 불면증	**regret** 후회하다, 유감이다

2. Let's Warm Up *Body Parts*

How many body parts do you know? Write down as many body parts as you can.

1. ______________ 2. ______________
3. ______________ 4. ______________
5. ______________ 6. ______________
7. ______________ 8. ______________
9. ______________ 10. ______________
11. ______________ 12. ______________

3. Conversation 1 *Aches and Pains*

Listen to the conversation. Then, practice it with a partner.

Nancy: Minho, you look terrible! What's wrong with you?
Minho: I have a cold. I feel awful.
Nancy: That's too bad. I'm sorry.
Minho: I also have a fever.
Nancy: Do you have a sore throat?
Minho: No, I don't. My throat doesn't hurt
Nancy: You need to see a doctor.
Minho: That's a good idea. Thanks.

Nancy: 민호야, 안 좋아 보인다. 왜 그러니?
Minho: 감기 걸렸어. 상태가 아주 나빠.
Nancy: 안 됐다. 어쩌니?
Minho: 열도 나.
Nancy: 목도 부었니?
Minho: 아니야. 목은 안 아파.
Nancy: 병원에 꼭 가 봐라.
Minho: 그러는 게 좋겠어. 고마워.

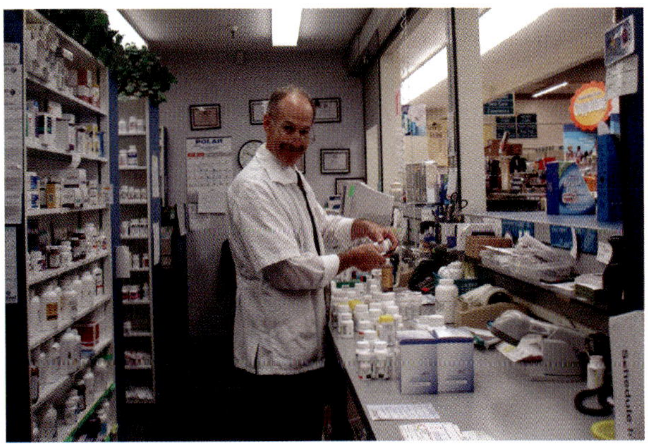

4. Let's Learn More 1

A *Look at the pictures.*

He has a headache.

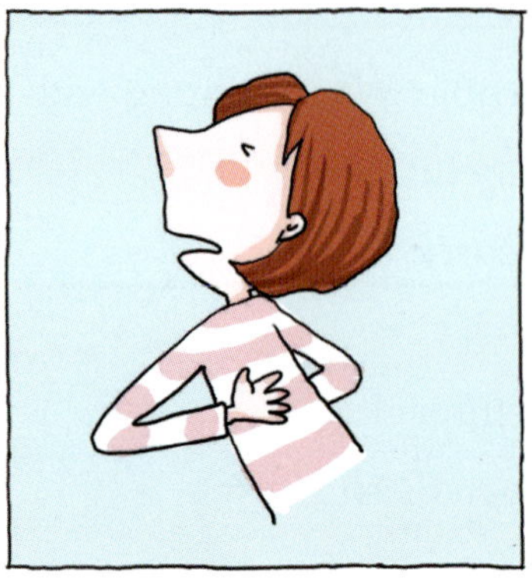

She has a backache.

He has a cough.

She has a sore throat.

She has a stomachache.

He has a fever.

He has a cold.

She has the flu.

He has insomnia.

B *Read the information below.*

There are usually three ways to talk about sicknesses or pain.

I have a ______.	My ______ hurts.	I have a sore ______.
headache	arm	eye
earache	foot	throat
stomachache	neck	knee
backache	back	back

C *Make sentences with the words below. Then, practice them with your partner.*

Q: What's wrong with Sumi?
A: Sumi has a sore throat.

1. Sumi/throat Q: A:	2. Tina/back Q: A:
3. Changhoon/leg Q: A:	4. Nancy/head Q: A:
5. Mark/arm Q: A:	6. Sujin/shoulder Q: A:

D *Match the symptoms with the health problems.*

1. ______ Mark's stomach feels bad.
2. ______ Sumi's throat hurts.
3. ______ Changhoon has a hot forehead.
4. ______ Tina can't move her back.
5. ______ Nancy just touched a very hot stove.
6. ______ Sujin cannot sleep at night.

A. He has a fever.
B. She has a backache.
C. She has insomnia.
D. She has a sore throat.
E. He has a stomachache.
F. She has a burn.

5. Conversation 2 *Conjunctions*

Sumi: Are you okay, Jason?
Jason: No, I'm not.
Sumi: What's the matter with you?
Jason: I have a headache, and I have a sore throat.
Sumi: That's not good.
Do you have a cold or the flu?
Jason: I have a cold, but I don't have the flu.
Sumi: Are you going to school or staying home?
Jason: I'm staying home today.
I need some rest.

Sumi: 제이슨, 너 괜찮니?
Jason: 아니, 괜찮지 않아.
Sumi: 왜 그러는데?
Jason: 머리가 아파.
목도 부어서 아프고.
Sumi: 안 됐구나.
감기나 독감에 걸린 거니?
Jason: 감기에 걸렸는데, 열은 없어.
Sumi: 학교에 갈래, 아니면 집에 있을래?
Jason: 오늘은 집에 있을래.
좀 쉬어야겠어.

6. Let's Learn More 2

A *Read the information below.*

Combine two sentences with conjunctions(접속사). Conjunctions are words like **and**, **but**, and **or**. Make sentences with them like this:

- I have a headache. I also have a backache.
  = I have a headache and a backache.
- Sumi has a cold. She doesn't have a sore throat.
  = Sumi has a cold, but she doesn't have a sore throat.
- Do you have a stomachache? Do you have a cold?
  = Do you have a stomachache or a cold? OR Do you have a stomachache, or do you have cold?

B *Use **and**, **but**, and **or** to combine the sentences.*

1. Jason has a cold. Jason also has a sore throat.

   = ______________________________

2. Sujin's back hurts. Her eye doesn't hurt.

   = ______________________________

3. Does Changhoon have a stomachache? Does he have a headache?

   = ______________________________

4. Nancy has a sore leg. She doesn't have a sore arm.

   = ______________________________

5. Mark has a computer. Mark has a car.

   = ______________________________

6. Mr. Kim enjoys sports. He doesn't enjoy computer games.

   = ______________________________

7. Does she know French? Does she know English?

   = ______________________________

8. I like English. I don't like math.

   = ______________________________

C *Complete the sentences with the correct conjunctions.*

1. He has a cough, __________ he doesn't have a cold.
2. My back hurts, __________ my legs hurt, too.
3. Hyoju has insomnia, __________ she also has a fever.
4. Do you have an earache __________ a sore eye?
5. I have a headache __________ not a stomachache.
6. Her neck is sore, __________ her legs are not.

D *Make sentences with the words below. Then, practice them with your partner.*

> *Q*: What's wrong with you?
> *A*: I have a backache, and my throat hurts.

1. back / throat Q: A:	2. eye / leg Q: A:
3. fever / cold Q: A:	4. insomnia / the flu Q: A:
5. knee / arm Q: A:	6. head / ear Q: A:

7. Let's Learn About Culture

A *Read the passage.*

In American culture, people often say, "I'm sorry." However, "I'm sorry," can have a couple of meanings. The first one is an apology. For example, you might do something wrong, or maybe you made a mistake. You should say, "I'm sorry." The second one is an expression of regret. For example, you might hear some bad news. Maybe your friend has a cold, or maybe your friend got a bad grade on a test. In these cases, you can also say, "I'm sorry." Here, you are not apologizing. You are telling the person you understand how badly he feels.

미국 문화에서는 사람들이 "I'm sorry."라는 말을 자주 한다. 그런데 "I'm sorry."는 두 가지의 의미를 지닌다. 첫 번째 것은 사과다. 예를 들어, 우리는 잘못을 하거나 실수를 저지를 수 있다. 그럴 때는 "I'm sorry."라고 말해야 한다. 두 번째 것은 유감의 표시다. 예를 들어, 우리는 나쁜 소식을 접할 수 있다. 친구가 감기에 걸렸다거나 시험 성적이 나쁘게 나왔을 수도 있다. 그런 경우에도 "I'm sorry."라고 말할 수 있는데, 이때는 사과하는 것이 아니다. 그 상대방의 기분이 좋지 않다는 것을 여러분도 느낀다는 점을 표현하는 것이다.

B *Are the sentences "I'm sorry" expressions of apology (A) or regret (R) in American culture? Write the answers.*

1. ______ A: I just broke up with my girlfriend. B: I'm sorry.
2. ______ A: Hey! You just hit me! B: I'm sorry.
3. ______ A: Be careful. You dropped that book on my foot. B: I'm sorry about that.
4. ______ A: I got an F on my math test. B: I'm sorry to hear that.

8. Use Your Knowledge

A *Look at the picture.*

B *Answer the questions. Then, practice them with your partner.*

1. What's the matter with Mark? ______________________
2. What's the matter with Jason? ______________________
3. What's the matter with Tina? ______________________
4. What's the matter with Nancy? ______________________
5. What's wrong with Changhoon? ______________________
6. What's wrong with Minho? ______________________
7. What's wrong with Sumi? ______________________
8. What's wrong with Sujin? ______________________

Unit 9

What does your brother look like?

1. Vocabulary

look ~하게 보이다
grandmother 할머니
clothes/clothing 옷/의류
ponytail 말총머리
best friend 가장 친한 친구
good-looking/handsome 잘 생긴
height 키
pretty 예쁜
wear 입다
picture 그림, 사진
wavy 구불구불한
medium (average) height 보통 키
middle-aged 중년의
curly 곱슬머리의
style 스타일, 문체
How tall ~? ~는 키가 얼마나 큰가요?
What does ~ look like? ~는 어떻게 생겼니?
button-down shirt 목 칼라에 단추를 채우는 와이셔츠
What kind of hair does ~ have? ~는 머리가 어떤 스타일이니?
blouse 블라우스
necklace 목걸이
Exactly. 맞아요.
accessory 액세서리
straight 곧은, 생머리의
description 묘사, 설명
clothes maker 의복 제작자

2. Let's Warm Up *Looks and Clothes*

Look at the picture. What do they look like? What are they wearing?

Woman

Looks:

Clothes:

Man

Looks:

Clothes:

3. Conversation 1 *Looks*

Listen to the conversation. Then, practice it with a partner.

Sumi: What does your brother look like?
Mark: He's really tall, and he's good looking.
Sumi: What kind of hair does he have?
Mark: He has short, straight brown hair. What about your sister?
Sumi: She looks pretty. Here is a picture of her.
Mark: Wow. She looks great, and I like her hair.
Sumi: Yeah, she has long, wavy black hair.

Sumi: 네 형은 어떻게 생겼니?
Mark: 키가 아주 크고 잘생겼어.
Sumi: 머리는 어떤 스타일인데?
Mark: 짧은 갈색머리야.
네 언니는?
Sumi: 예쁘게 생겼어.
여기 우리 언니 사진 있어.
Mark: 우와. 멋지게 생겼다.
그리고 머리 스타일도 참 좋다.
Sumi: 응, 머리가 길고
구불구불한 검정색이지.

4. Let's Learn More 1

A *Look at the pictures. Practice the sentences with your partner.*

She's tall.

He's medium height.

She's short.

He's young.

He's middle aged.

She's old.

She's pretty.

He's handsome.

They're good looking.

She has long, wavy black hair.

He has short, straight brown hair.

She has medium-length, curly blond hair.

B *Answer the questions. Then, talk with your partner.*

1. How tall are you? ____________________
2. How tall is your brother / sister? ____________________
3. How old are you? ____________________
4. How old is your grandmother? ____________________
5. What do you look like? ____________________
6. What does your mother look like? ____________________
7. What kind of hair do you have? ____________________
8. What kind of hair does your father have? ____________________

C *Match the sentences.*

1. Jason is 190 centimeters tall.
2. Minho is a handsome man.
3. Her mother is 45 years old.
4. Sumi is 150 centimeters tall.
5. Mark has no hair.
6. My father is 67 years old.
7. Wendy is a pretty woman.
8. Sujin has long, straight hair.

A. He's bald.
B. She's short.
C. She also has a ponytail.
D. He's old.
E. She is very beautiful.
F. He is very tall.
G. He's really good looking.
H. She is middle aged.

D *Answer the questions.*

Think about your best friend.

1. How tall is he / she? ____________________
2. How old is he / she? ____________________
3. What does he / she look like? ____________________
4. What kind of hair does he / she have? ____________________

E *Ask and answer questions about looks with your partners. Write the answers.*

	Student 1	Student 2	Student 3
Height			
Age			
Looks			
Hair			

5. Conversation 2 *Clothes*

Jason: Where is Sujin? I can't see her.
Minho: She is standing with those two women.
Jason: What is she wearing?
Minho: She is wearing a white blouse and blue jeans.
Jason: I think I see her. Is she wearing a blue sweater and a gold necklace, too?
Minho: No, that's Hyoju. Sujin isn't wearing a necklace or a sweater.
Jason: Then Sujin is wearing black heels and glasses, right?
Minho: Exactly. That's Sujin.

Jason: 수진이 어디 있니? 걔를 볼 수가 없네.
Minho: 저 두 여성들과 같이 서 있어.
Jason: 뭘 입고 있는데?
Minho: 흰 블라우스와 청바지를 입고 있어.
Jason: 찾은 것 같아. 청색 스웨터와 금목걸이도 하고 있니?
Minho: 아니, 그건 효주야. 수진이는 목걸이를 하고 있지 않아.
Jason: 그럼 수진이는 검정색 힐을 신고 안경을 썼구나. 그렇지?
Minho: 맞았어. 그게 수진이야.

6. Let's Learn More 2

A *Look at the pictures. Practice the sentences with your partner.*

(polo) shirt

T-shirt

blouse

button-down shirt
dress shirt

pants

(blue) jeans

(mini) skirt

shorts

shoes

tennis shoes
sneakers

(high) heels

sandals

jacket

suit

sweater

cap

B *Answer the questions.*

1. What are you wearing? ______________________
2. What kind of shirt are you wearing? ______________________
3. What kind of pants are you wearing? ______________________
4. What kind of shoes are you wearing? ______________________
5. What accessories are you wearing? ______________________

C *Ask and answer questions about your clothes with your partners. Write the answers.*

What ~ are you wearing?	Student 1	Student 2	Student 3
kind of shirt			
kind of pants			
kind of shoes			
accessories			

7. Let's Learn About Culture

A Read the passage.

When people talk about clothes, they usually talk about shirts, pants, and shoes. BUT... Don't say, "I am wearing a shirt, pants, and shoes." You need to give more description. You should say the style and the color. Look at these examples:

Bad Description	Good Description
Jason is wearing shoes.	*Jason is wearing black dress shoes.*
Sumi is wearing a dress.	*Sumi is wearing a blue dress.*
Changhoon is wearing a T-shirt.	*Changhoon is wearing a short-sleeved T-shirt.*

In addition, don't talk about the price of your clothes. In American culture, that is rude. However, give the name of the clothes maker. You can say, "It's a Polo shirt," "She's wearing a Gucci dress," or, "He has a Rolex watch."

사람들은 의류에 관해서 얘기할 때 주로 윗도리, 바지, 신발 등에 관해서 얘기한다. 그런데 이때 단순히 "나는 셔츠를 입었다.", "바지를 입고 있다.", "신발을 신고 있다." 이런 식으로 말해서는 안 된다. 좀 더 설명을 붙여서 말해야 한다. 즉, 스타일과 색상에 대해서 말해줘야 한다. 다음의 예를 살펴보자.

좋지 않은 설명	좋은 설명
제이슨은 신발을 신고 있다.	제이슨은 검정색 정장 신발을 신고 있다.
수미는 드레스를 입고 있다.	수미는 파란색 드레스를 입고 있다.
창훈이는 티셔츠를 입고 있다.	창훈이는 반소매 티셔츠를 입고 있다.

또한 옷값에 대해서 얘기하지 말 것! 미국 문화에서 그것은 실례가 된다. 하지만 브랜드는 얘기해줄 수 있다. "그건 폴로 셔츠야.", "그 여자는 구찌 드레스를 입었다." 또는 "그 남자가 롤렉스 시계를 가졌네." 정도는 말할 수 있다.

B Are these good (G) or bad (B) descriptions of clothes? Write the answers.

1. ________ Sujin is wearing a red miniskirt.
2. ________ Minho is wearing a shirt and jeans.
3. ________ Nancy is wearing a $100 bracelet.
4. ________ Jason is wearing blue jeans, white sneakers, and a red baseball cap.
5. ________ Tina is wearing a gold necklace and diamond earrings.
6. ________ Changhoon is wearing a Nike T-shirt.

8. Use Your Knowledge

A *Look at the picture.*

B *Complete the questions and answers. Then, practice them with your partner.*

1. What does Sumi look like?

2. What is Sumi wearing?

3. What does Tina look like?

4. What is Tina wearing?

5. What does Changhoon look like?

6. What is Changhoon wearing?

Unit 10 Italian food is more delicious than Chinese food.

1. Vocabulary

comparison 비교	**smart** 머리가 좋은
low 낮은	**silk** 비단
high 높은	**sandpaper** 사포
fun 재미(있는)	**smooth** 매끄러운
famous 유명한	**forget** 잊다
fascinating 매혹적인	**amazing** 대단한, 놀라운
similarity 유사성	**difference** 차이점
disappointing 실망스러운	**mean** 의미하다, 못되게 굴다
delightful 기쁜, 마음이 밝은	**funny** 재미있는, 웃기는
energetic 힘이 넘치는	**adjective** 형용사
exhausting 지치게 만드는	**taste** 맛, ~한 맛이 나다
rainy 비가 오락가락하는	**prefer** 더 좋아하다

Do you like ~ or ~? 너는 ~가 좋으니, 아니면 ~가 좋으니?

2. Let's Warm Up *Making Comparisons*

Circle the correct answers.

1. Mount Everest is (lower / higher) than Seorak Mountain.
2. Puppies are (cuter / uglier) than snakes.
3. Korean food is (better / worse) than Mexican food.
4. English is (more fun / less fun) than math.
5. A mouse is (smaller / bigger) than an elephant.

3. Conversation 1 *Comparisons with -er*

Listen to the conversation. Then, practice it with a partner.

Jason: I love the zoo.
I always have a great time here.
Sumi: Do you like the monkeys or the elephants?
Jason: Well, the monkeys are funnier than the elephants.
Sumi: That's true. But the elephants are bigger than the monkeys.
Jason: I've got an idea.
Let's see the lions.
Sumi: Great! The lions are cuter than the monkeys.
Jason: Cuter? Are you joking?
Sumi: No, they look like my cats.
But they're larger than my cats.

Jason: 난 동물원이 좋아.
여기 오면 언제나 즐거워.
Sumi: 넌 원숭이가 좋으니, 아니면 코끼리가 좋으니?
Jason: 글쎄, 원숭이가 코끼리보다 더 웃겨.
Sumi: 그건 맞아. 하지만 코끼리가 원숭이보다 더 크지.
Jason: 나한테 한 가지 생각이 있어.
사자를 보러 가자.
Sumi: 그래! 사자는 원숭이보다 더 귀엽지.
Jason: 더 귀여워? 지금 농담하니?
Sumi: 아니, 사자는 내 고양이처럼 생겼어.
하지만 내 고양이보다는 더 크지.

4. Let's Learn More 1

A *Read the information below.*

Use comparisons to talk about the similarities and differences between two people, things, or ideas. Form comparisons like this:

adjective + -er

big → bigger	mean → meaner	hot → hotter
small → smaller	young → younger	cold → colder
nice → nicer	old → older	good → better

B *Write the comparative form of each adjective.*

1. clean → ____________ 2. kind→ ____________
3. happy → ____________ 4. sad → ____________
5. pretty → ____________ 6. ugly → ____________
7. tall → ____________ 8. short → ____________
9. good → ____________ 10. warm→ ____________
11. cool → ____________ 12. funny→ ____________

C *Read the information below.*

Make comparisons in some sentences like this:

A + verb + adjective + than + B

1. Summer is hotter than winter.
2. My best friend is older than me.
3. The boy is shorter than the man.
4. Girls are nicer than boys.
5. Strawberries taste better than apples.
6. Rock music sounds louder than classical music.

D *Make comparisons with the words below. Then, say them with your partner.*

A rabbit is faster than a turtle.

1. rabbit / turtle / be / fast	2. spring / summer / be / cool
3. computer / sports car / be / cheap	4. summer / fall / be / rainy
5. Bill Gates / me / be / rich	6. Tina / Nancy / be / smart
7. my mother / chef / cook / good	8. silk / sandpaper / feel / smooth

5. Conversation 2 *Comparisons with More*

Sujin: Who's your favorite movie star?
Nancy: I love Brad Pitt. He's really handsome.
Sujin: That's true. But Dwayne Johnson is more handsome than Brad Pitt.
Nancy: You're right. I forgot about him.
Sujin: Hey, I'm hungry. Let's eat lunch now.
Nancy: All right. Do you want Italian or Chinese food?
Sujin: Italian food is more delicious than Chinese food.
Nancy: I agree. Let's find an Italian restaurant.

Sujin: 네가 제일 좋아하는 영화배우는 누구니?
Nancy: 난 브래드 피트를 무척 좋아해. 정말 잘생겼잖아.
Sujin: 그래, 하지만 드웨인 존슨이 브래드 피트보다 더 잘생겼어.
Nancy: 네 말이 맞아. 장동건을 잊고 있었네.
Sujin: 얘, 나 배고파. 이제 점심 먹자.
Nancy: 그래. 이탈리아 음식 먹을래, 아니면 중국 음식 먹을래?
Sujin: 이탈리아 음식이 중국 음식보다 더 맛있어.
Nancy: 맞아. 이탈리아 식당을 찾아보자.

6. Let's Learn More 2

A *Read the information below.*

You can make the comparative forms of long adjectives like this:

more + adjective

interesting → more interesting
beautiful → more beautiful
handsome → more handsome

fascinating → more fascinating
boring → more boring
amazing → more amazing

B *Write the comparative form of each adjective.*

1. pleasant → ______________________ 2. terrific→ ______________________
3. terrible → ______________________ 4. fun→ ______________________
5. disappointing → ______________________ 6. delightful→ ______________________
7. energetic → ______________________ 8. exhausting→ ______________________

C *Make comparisons with the words below. Then, say them with your partner.*

A dog is more energetic than a cat.

1. dog / cat / be / energetic	2. computer games / school / be / fun
3. computer / pencil / be / expensive	4. English / Korean / be / difficult
5. soccer / ping-pong / be / fun	6. running / watching TV / be / exhausting
7. sofa / chair / look / comfortable	8. medicine / candy / taste / terrible

D *Complete the sentences.*

1. I am ______________________ than my best friend.
2. My best friend is ______________________ than me.
3. I am ______________________ than my brother / sister.
4. My brother / sister is ______________________ than me.
5. Meeting my friends is ______________________ than studying.
6. Watching TV is ______________________ than reading books.
7. Computer games are ______________________ than sports.
8. Pets are ______________________ than people.

E Read the information below.

Use **prefer** to ask a person about two choices. Look at the following examples:

Do you prefer summer or winter?	I prefer summer to winter. I like summer more than winter. I like both. / I like neither. / I don't like either.
Which do you prefer, dogs or cats?	I prefer dogs to cats. I like dogs more than cats. I like both. / I like neither. / I don't like either.

F Answer the questions. Use comparisons.

1. Do you prefer strawberry ice cream or chocolate ice cream?

2. Do you prefer airplanes or cars?

3. Do you prefer spring or fall?

4. Do you prefer English or Korean?

5. Which do you prefer, studying math or playing soccer?

6. Which do you prefer, cooking or eating?

7. Which do you prefer, going out or staying home?

8. Which do you prefer, shopping at stores or shopping on the Internet?

7. Let's Learn About Culture

A Read the passage.

When Americans talk about their preferences, they use many different expressions. Sometimes they say, "I like it," "I like it a lot," "I don't like it," or "I don't like it very much." However, many Americans use strong expressions. For example, they might say, "I love it," or, "I hate it." Do not be shocked by these expressions. Even though they are strong, they just mean, "I like it very much," and "I dislike it very much." Here are some other strong positive and negative expressions:

Positive Expressions	Negative Expressions
That rules!	*I can't stand that.*
It's awesome.	*That's awful.*
It's the best.	*That's the worst.*

미국인들은 자기가 좋아하는 것을 말할 때 다양한 표현을 사용한다. 때로는 "I like it," "I like it a lot," "I don't like it," 또는 "I don't like it very much." 이런 표현을 사용한다. 하지만 미국 사람들 중에는 아주 강한 표현을 쓰는 사람들이 많다. 예를 들어 "I love it," 또는 "I hate it." 이런 표현을 쓰는 경우도 있는데, 이런 표현 때문에 충격을 받을 필요는 없다. 이런 표현들은 강한 표현이긴 하지만, 그냥 "난 그걸 무척 좋아한다." 또는 "난 그걸 무척 싫어한다."는 뜻일 뿐이다. 이와 같이 강한 긍정과 부정의 표현들 중에는 다음과 같은 것들도 있다.

긍정적인 표현들	부정적인 표현들
That rules!	I can't stand that.
It's awesome.	That's awful.
It's the best.	That's the worst.

B Are these sentences positive (P) or negative (N)? Write the answers.

1. __________ I love cheesecake.
2. __________ Mexican food is the worst.
3. __________ American football rules!
4. __________ Dogs are awesome.
5. __________ I can't stand waking up early.
6. __________ Horror movies are awful.
7. __________ My English teacher is the best.

8. Use Your Knowledge

A *Look at the picture.*

B *Write the questions and answers. Then, practice them with your partner.*

1. (height) *Who is taller, Jason or Mark?* ______ *Jason is taller than Mark.*
2. (looks) ______ ______
3. (hair) ______ ______
4. (money) ______ ______
5. (clothes) ______ ______
6. (grades) ______ ______

Unit 11
I will have dinner after class.

1. Vocabulary

future 미래	**Awesome.** 멋지다. 좋아.
after class 수업 끝나고	**Wow.** 우와
I'm starving. 나 배고파.	**have a ~ time** ~한 시간을 보내다.
plans 할 일, 계획	**great** 대단한, 훌륭한
yet 아직, 벌써	**I hope so.** 그랬으면 좋겠어.
then 그러면, 그러자	**Nothing.** 아무 일도 아니야.
Sure. 그래, 그럼	**common** 흔히 있는, 보통의
future simple tense 단순 미래시제	**take a break** 잠시 쉬다
take a trip 여행하다	**marry** 결혼하다
hard 열심히, 어려운, 딱딱한	**want to** ~하고 싶다
graduate 졸업하다	**desire** 원하다, 갈망하다
vacation 방학, 휴가	**find** 찾아내다
come 오다	**definitely** 그래, 결정적으로
I'm so ~ 나는 매우 ~하다.	**absolutely** 맞아, 절대적으로

2. Let's Warm Up *Future Schedule*

Write down your schedule for next week.

Monday:

Tuesday

Wednesday:

Thursday:

Friday:

Saturday:

Sunday:

3. Conversation 1 *The Future with Will*

Listen to the conversation. Then, practice it with a partner.

Sumi: What will you do after class?
Jason: I will have dinner after class. I'm starving.
Sumi: Who will you eat with?
Jason: I don't have any plans yet.
Sumi: Then will you have dinner with me?
Jason: Sure. I can do that.
Sumi: I will meet some friends at 6:00. We can all eat together.
Jason: Excellent. I can't wait.

Sumi: 수업 끝나고 뭐할 거니?
Jason: 수업 끝나면 저녁 먹을 거야. 나 엄청 배고파.
Sumi: 누구랑 먹을 건데?
Jason: 아직 별다른 계획은 없어.
Sumi: 그럼 너 나랑 같이 먹을래?
Jason: 그래. 그럴 수 있어.
Sumi: 내가 친구들을 여섯 시에 만나거든. 우리 다 같이 먹자.
Jason: 좋아. 어서 먹었으면 좋겠다.

4. Let's Learn More 1

A *Read the information below.*

Use the future simple tense to talk about future events or actions. Form the future simple tense like this:

will + verb

I will take a trip tomorrow.
He will watch a movie later.
You will study hard tonight.
We will eat dinner at 6:00.
Sumi will meet her friends this weekend.
They will graduate next year.

B *Answer the questions. Then, talk with your partner.*

1. What will you do tonight? ______________________
2. What will you do tomorrow? ______________________
3. What will your family do this weekend? ______________________
4. What will your friends do next week? ______________________
5. Where will your friends go after class? ______________________
6. What will you eat for dinner? ______________________
7. Who will you talk to tonight? ______________________
8. When will your teacher give you a test? ______________________

C *Read the information below. Then, answer the questions.*

Time expressions are very important for the future tense. Always use time expressions with the future tense. Here are some future time words:

tonight 오늘 밤, 오늘 저녁 **tomorrow** 내일
tomorrow morning/afternoon/evening/night 내일 아침/오후/저녁/밤
next Monday 다음 주 월요일 **next weekend** 다음 주말
next week 다음 주 **next month/year** 다음 달/내년
this Friday 이번 주 금요일 **this weekend** 이번 주말
later 나중에 **soon** 곧
in 20 minutes/20 minutes from now 20분 후에

D *Ask and answer the questions with your partner. Write the answers.*

What will you do ~?	Student 1	Student 2	Student 3
after class			
tomorrow morning			
tomorrow evening			
this weekend			

5. Conversation 2 *The Future with Be Going To*

Minho: Vacation is coming soon. I'm so happy.
Tina: What are you going to do this vacation?
Minho: I'm going to take a trip this vacation.
Tina: Great. Where are you going to go?
Minho: I'm going to go to the United States.
Tina: Awesome. You're going to have a great time.
Minho: I hope so. What are you going to do?
Tina: Nothing. I'm going to stay home.

Minho: 방학이 곧 다가온다. 난 너무 기뻐.
Tina: 이번 방학 때는 뭐할 거니?
Minho: 난 이번 방학 때 여행을 할 거야.
Tina: 좋겠다. 어디로 갈 건데?
Minho: 미국으로 갈 거야.
Tina: 멋지다. 아주 좋은 시간이 되겠는걸.
Minho: 그랬으면 좋겠어. 넌 뭐할 거니?
Tina: 아무것도 안 할 거야. 그냥 집에 있을 거야.

6. Let's Learn More 2

A *Read the information below.*

There is another common way to make the future tense in English. Make it like this:

be + going to + verb
(am, is, are)

I am going to learn Russian next year.
You are going to meet my family tonight.
She is going to take a break soon.
We are going to finish class in 5 minutes.

B Answer the questions. Then talk with your partner.

1. What are you going to do tomorrow? ______________________
2. What are you going to do tonight? ______________________
3. What are your friends going to do next week?
____
4. What is your best friend going to study tomorrow?
____
5. What movie is your family going to watch soon?
____
6. When are you going to go home today? ______________________
7. Who are you going to meet this weekend? ______________________
8. How are you going to go to school tomorrow?
____

C Circle the mistakes. Then, write the correct sentences.

1. Minsu is going to going home soon. → ______________________
2. Tina are going to make dinner. → ______________________
3. We are will do our homework tonight. → ______________________
4. What are you go to do later? → ______________________
5. Nancy is going surf the Internet later. → ______________________
6. When she going to take a break? → ______________________

D Ask and answer the questions with your partner. Write the answers.

What are you going to ~?	Student 1	Student 2	Student 3
eat tonight			
study tomorrow			
watch later			
do next week			

E *Read the information below. Then, answer the questions.*

Another way to talk about the future is to use **want to**. This is a desire or wish for the future. Use it in sentences like this:

want to + verb

I want to go home now.
We want to do well on our test next week.
Changhoon wants to be a doctor in the future.
They want to take a trip this weekend.
She wants to meet her best friend tonight.

F *Answer the questions. Then, talk with your partner.*

1. What do you want to be in the future? ______________________
2. What do you want to do tomorrow? ______________________
3. What do your classmates want to eat later?
____
4. Where does your family want to go this vacation?
____
5. Who does your teacher want to talk to? ______________________
6. When do you want to find a job? ______________________

F *Complete the sentences.*

1. Today, I want to ______________________.
2. Tomorrow, I want to ______________________.
3. This weekend, my brother/sister wants to ______________________.
4. Next week, my teacher wants to ______________________.
5. I want to ______________________ next year.
6. My best friend wants to ______________________ in the future.
7. I want to ______________________ in 5 minutes.
8. My mother/father wants to ______________________ soon.

7. Let's Learn About Culture

A *Read the passage.*

You can use both **will** and **be going to** to talk about the future. BUT they are a little different from each other. Use **will** to talk about an action in the future you are not sure about. In other words, maybe you will do it, or maybe you won't. You can use the words *perhaps*, *maybe*, and *probably* with **will**. However, use **be going to** to talk about an action in the future you are 100% going to do. You can use the words *definitely* or *absolutely* with **be going to**. In addition, use **will** to talk about an action that you just decided to do right now.

미래를 말할 때 will과 be going to를 모두 사용할 수 있다. 그러나 이 두 표현은 서로 다른 점이 있다. 확실하지 않은 미래의 행동을 말할 때는 will을 사용한다. 다시 말해서 will을 사용하면 그 일을 할 수도 있고 안 할 수도 있다. 따라서 will과 함께 perhaps, maybe, probably를 사용하는 경우가 많다. 미래에 반드시 할 행동을 말할 때는 be going to를 사용한다. 따라서 be going to와 함께 definitely 또는 absolutely 같은 말을 할 수가 있다. 또한 지금 막 마음먹은 행동을 말할 때 will을 사용한다.

B *Do these sentences need **will** or **be going to**? Circle the answers.*

1. The phone is ringing. I (will / am going to) answer it.
2. My brother definitely (will / is going to) attend college next year.
3. It (will / is going to) rain tomorrow. I am sure of it.
4. Maybe Jason (will / is going to) buy a present for Sumi tomorrow.
5. I don't know. Perhaps I (will / am going to) watch a movie tonight.
6. They (will / are going to) come around nine. They promised me.
7. She (will / is going to) probably take the job in Daegu.
8. Absolutely! We (will / are going to) meet everyone in front of the school.

8. Use Your Knowledge

A *Look at the pictures.*

Monday

Tuesday

Wednesday

Thursday

Friday

Saturday

Sunday

Sunday

B *Complete the questions and answers. Then, practice them with your partner.*

1. *What will Sumi do on Monday?* ______________________
2. *What will Sumi* ______________________
3. ______________________ ______________________
4. ______________________ ______________________
5. ______________________ ______________________
6. ______________________ ______________________
7. ______________________ ______________________
8. ______________________ ______________________

Unit 12
I have to make hotel reservations.

1. Vocabulary

requirement 필수요건, 필수과목
visit 찾아가다
visa 입국사증
have to 반드시 ~해야 한다
What else ~? 그 밖에 또 무엇을 ~하시나요?
make a reservation 예약하다
must 반드시 ~해야 한다
obligation 의무
be quiet 조용히 하다
find a job 직장을 구하다
be careful 주의하다
buy 사다
wonderful 훌륭한
worried 걱정되는
safe 안전한
should ~하는 게 좋다
advice 충고, 조언
Have a great ~ 좋은 ~되세요.
ought to ~하는 게 좋다
leave 떠나다, 뒤에 남기다
attend 참석하다
need 꼭 필요하다
forget 잊어버리다
passport 여권
finally 마침내
imperative 명령문, 강제적인, 절박한
order 명령, 질서, 주문
demand 요구하다

2. Let's Warm Up *Daily Requirements*

What do you have to do every day?

Morning:
Afternoon:
Evening:
Night:

3. Conversation 1 *Have to and Must*

Listen to the conversation. Then, practice it with a partner.

Mark: You're going to visit the United States, right?
Minho: Yes, I'm going to go there next month.
Mark: Do you have a visa?
Minho: Yes, I have to have a visa.
Mark: What else do you have to do?
Minho: Hmm. I have to make hotel reservations.
Mark: Yeah. And you have to bring U.S. dollars.
Minho: That's right. I must have American money there.

Mark: 너 미국 갈 거지, 그렇지?
Minho: 응, 다음 달에 갈 거야.
Mark: 비자는 있니?
Minho: 응, 난 비자가 있어야 돼.
Mark: 그 밖에는 뭘 해야 되니?
Minho: 흠. 호텔 예약을 해야 돼.
Mark: 그래. 그리고 미국 달러를 가져가야 된다.
Minho: 맞아. 그곳에서는 미국 돈이 있어야지.

4. Let's Learn More 1

A *Read the information below.*

Use **have to** and **must** to talk about **requirements** or **obligations**. Use them in sentences like this:

have to + verb	must + verb
I have to call my parents now.	I must find a job soon.
She has to work harder.	He must go to class now.
We have to be quiet.	They must be more careful.

B *Answer the questions. Then, talk with your partner.*

1. What do you have to do every day? ______________________
2. Where do you have to go tomorrow? ______________________
3. When does your brother/sister have to work?

   ____
4. Who do you have to meet soon? ______________________
5. What must your class do next week? ______________________
6. Where must your partner go after class? ______________________
7. When must you go home today? ______________________
8. Who must you call later? ______________________

C *Answer T (true) or F (false) to the following questions.*

1. ________ I have to go home by ten every night.
2. ________ I have to do homework every day.
3. ________ I have to cook dinner at my home every day.
4. ________ I must wake up at six every morning.
5. ________ I must take a test next week.
6. ________ I must go to school tomorrow morning.

D *Ask and answer the following questions. Write the answers.*

What do you have to ~?	Student 1	Student 2	Student 3
do tonight			
study tomorrow			
buy this week			
finish soon			

5. Conversation 2 *Should and Ought To*

Sumi: I will visit Thailand this vacation.

Nancy: That's great news. You'll have a wonderful time there.

Sumi: Yes, but I'm worried. Is it safe?

Nancy: Yes, it is. But you should be careful.

Sumi: That's good advice.

Nancy: And you should go with a friend.

Sumi: Right. I'm going to go there with Tina.

Nancy: Have a wonderful trip.

Sumi: 난 이번 방학 때 태국에 갈 거야.

Nancy: 좋은 소식이로군. 거기서 좋은 시간이 될 거야.

Sumi: 응, 그런데 걱정이 돼. 안전할까?

Nancy: 응. 하지만 조심하는 게 좋지.

Sumi: 좋은 충고야.

Nancy: 그리고 넌 친구랑 같이 가는 게 좋을 거야.

Sumi: 맞아. 난 그곳에 티나랑 같이 갈 거야.

Nancy: 잘 다녀와.

6. Let's Learn More 2

A *Read the information below.*

Use **should** and **ought to** to talk about something that is NOT a requirement but is a *good idea* to do. Use them in sentences like this:

should + verb	ought to + verb
I should leave now. (But I do not have to.)	I ought to call my friend soon.
You should talk to Tina.	You ought to buy that.
We should have lunch now.	They ought to attend class now.

B *Answer the questions. Then, talk to your partner.*

1. What should you do this afternoon? ______________________
2. When should your partner go to school? ______________________
3. What time should you have lunch? ______________________
4. Who should you ask for advice? ______________________
5. Where should your brother/sister go tomorrow?
____
6. What ought you to do later? ______________________
7. What class ought you to attend today? ______________________
8. Where ought your family to go this vacation?
____

C *Complete the sentences.*

1. I have class soon. I should ______________________.
2. My friend has a problem. I should ______________________.
3. My friend has no money. I should ______________________.
4. I feel sick. I ought to ______________________.
5. I am not good at English. I ought to ______________________.
6. My brother needs a job. I ought to ______________________.

D *Ask and answer the following questions. Write the answers.*

What should you ~?	Student 1	Student 2	Student 3
do later			
eat soon			
study harder			
forget about			

E *Read the information below. Then, write the answers.*

You are planning a trip to the United States. What do you have to do? What should you do?

	Have to / Must	Should / Ought to
1.	*I have to get a passport.*	*I should buy a map of the United States.*
2.		
3.		
4.		
5.		
6.		
7.		
8.		

F *Complete the sentences.*

1. Before I go to the United States. first, I have to ______________.
2. Then, I should ______________.
3. I must also ______________.
4. In the United States , I ought to ______________.
5. And I have to ______________.
6. Finally, I should ______________.

7. Let's Learn About Culture

A *Read the passage.*

A lot of people use imperatives in English. Imperatives are orders or demands. There are many common imperatives. Here are some of them:

Be quiet.
Sit down.
Open your books.
Stop it.
Get away from me.
Don't do that.

Imperatives always begin with a verb. The subject is "you," but you do NOT say "you." However, you must be careful with imperatives. Sometimes they may sound very rude. Your tone of voice is very important. You can also use the word "please." This will make your imperatives sound much nicer.

영어에서는 많은 사람들이 명령문을 사용한다. 명령문이란 명령이나 요구다. 흔히 사용되는 명령문이 많이 있는데, 그것들은 다음과 같다.

Be quiet. (조용히 해.)
Sit down. (앉아.)
Open your books. (책을 펴라.)
Stop it. (그만 해.)
Get away from me. (저리 가.)
Don't do that. (그러지 마.)

명령문은 언제나 동사부터 시작된다. 주어는 "you"지만 "you"라고 말하지는 않는다. 하지만 명령문을 사용할 때는 주의해야 한다. 때로 명령문이 아주 무례한 말로 들릴 수가 있기 때문이다. 말투도 매우 중요하다. 또한 "please"를 붙여서 말해야 할 때도 있다. 그렇게 하면 명령 표현이 훨씬 친절하게 들리기 때문이다.

B *Are these imperatives polite (P) or impolite (I) in American culture? Write the answers.*

1. ________ Shut up!
2. ________ Please open the window.
3. ________ Listen carefully, please.
4. ________ Go home.
5. ________ Get out of here.
6. ________ Watch your step, please.
7. ________ Give me that!

8. Use Your Knowledge

A *Look at the picture.*

B *Complete the questions and answers. Then, practice them with your partner.*

1. *What should Sujin and Tina do for their trip?* ______ *They should* ______
2. *What must Sujin and Tina do for their trip?* ______ *They must* ______
3. ______ ______
4. ______ ______
5. ______ ______
6. ______ ______
7. ______ ______
8. ______ ______

저자 소개

Michael Putlack
Michael Putlack studied history and English at Tufts University in Medford, Massachusetts, USA, where he got his B.A. and M.A. He lives in Korea and currently teaches at Dongyang Technical College in Seoul.

이현호
서울 출생
동양공업전문대학 교수
대학입학 학력고사 출제위원
EBS교육방송 영어회화 프로그램 진행
알파시그마누(예수회 명예협회) 종신회원
Who'sWho in theWorld 세계인명사전 등재

Stephen Poirier
동양미래대학교 교양과 교수

New English Conversation Arts 1

초　판 1쇄 발행 / 2008년 8월 20일
개 정 판 1쇄 발행 / 2017년 8월 31일
개 정2판 1쇄 발행 / 2026년 1월 30일

공저　Michael Putlack · 이현호 · Stephen Poirier
발행처　형설출판사
경기도 파주시 회동길 37-23 · 전화 (031) 955-2361～4 · 팩시밀리 (031) 955-2341
발행인　장진혁
등록　라－제9호 · 1962년 5월 1일
홈페이지　http://www.hyungseul.co.kr
e-mail　hs@hyungseul.co.kr

정가 14,000원

ISBN 978-89-472-8813-2 93740